The Sea

The

Search

for Wisdom and Understanding

Proverbs 4:7 *"Wisdom is the principle thing; Therefore get wisdom.*
And in all your getting, get understanding." **NKJV**

by

Danny G. Thomas

II Cor. 4:1 & 2

Bible versions are from KJV, NKJV, ESV, NLT, LIVING BIBLE and
MESSAGE.
This book was printed in the United States of America.

To order additional copies of this book contact:

dannygthomas47@gmail.com

FWB
For Worthwhile Books Publications
Columbus, Ohio

Once again I dedicate another book to my lovely wife,
Bobbie.
She has been a source for added strength to my life
and a confidant whom I often go to as an intercessor in
prayer
in seeking God's wisdom and understanding.
I love you dearly!
Danny

Preface

Many times I have been awakened in the night with thoughts of God's Word, or an application of his Word, and thoughts of His goodness to me. I would have thoughts of how God was at work in my life leading me to do something for someone special who might benefit from it. I have learned that if I don't get up and write these thoughts down, they will be gone by morning.

Did you know that God often does this for all of us? I have found those thoughts in the night to be just what I needed for another day or something that I could share with someone else at a future God-appointed time. God's written Word is never given in vain, and these thoughts in the night are never given without a purpose.

In this ninety-day section, I have been challenged to share what God has given me with you, the reader, in mind. As you search for wisdom and seek understanding, I know that you will gain a greater insight of life as we focus on God's Word. My prayer is that the Holy Spirit will enlighten you and give you answers in your quest and search. To God be the glory and to Him alone.

In His service together,
Danny G. Thomas

Table of Contents

Day 1: Pressed

"Not that I have already obtained this or am already perfect, but I press on to make it my own, because Christ Jesus has made me his own. Brothers, I do not consider that I have made it my own. But one thing I do: forgetting what lies behind and straining forward to what lies ahead, I press on toward the goal for the prize of the upward call of God in Christ Jesus." **Philippians 3:12-14 ESV**

When we find ourselves battled, bruised, wounded and weary, our concern tends to turn inward. We begin to think, "Is this battle really worth all of this? Why is this happening anyway? What is the purpose? What's the point?

Having a good understanding is what causes us to be able to get over and through the battles, bruises and bumps in life. So, what are you fighting for? What is the purpose, the goal, the vision, or the point of it all? Who is our enemy and who is with us? Are we alone?

The wounds are from the war, and the war is against principalities, not people. We are fighting for Jesus. The point of it all is to obey our commander Jesus Christ, God's Son, and the mission we are on is to make disciples of the captive. The vision is a new homeland, a new earth, and to enjoy worship in a new heaven, the sanctuary of God Himself.

Some things to remember:

1. When God gives us a vision and darkness begins to hide God's face: *"Rest on His unchanging grace, when all around your soul gives way, He then is all your hope and stay."* **Edward Mote**

2. Wait for God to move. Don't get ahead or try to second-guess; just stand where you are.

3. Remember what God has told you to do. Remember your mission and stick to it.
   "God will bring the vision and mission to a reality in your life if you wait on His timing." **Oswald Chambers**

4. Never try to help God fulfill His Word. He does it and brings it to fulfillment.

5. Don't look at the blessings in the battle; look at the God who gave the blessing. If you look at the blessing, it could become more important than the mission.

Press on with Christ, forget the past, keep the faith, and receive the reward. You are more than just a victor; you are the child of the King. Don't get discouraged; get encouraged. If everything seems to be going wrong, it may be that things are about to start going right. Remember, God is in charge, not the discourager.

Think about it. *Selah!*

Day 2: Hindered

"Who has bewitched you?" **Galatians 3:1 ESV**

Has something been hindering you in your Christian life? You may feel it is some power, human or Satanic, which has prevented or hindered you from accomplishing what God has called you to do. It could be it is neither one. It could be the Holy Spirit leading you or directing you in another path. It could be the Holy Spirit behind you whispering to you, "No, that is not the road that I want you to take right now." **Isaiah 30:21**

What the Holy Spirit is doing is directing us to the right road, the right path, and the right direction that He would have us go. *"This is the way, walk in it."* **Isaiah 30:21 ESV**

The problem that we sometimes have is our desire, or our pick of a path based totally on our feeling. Don't put stock in feeling, but rather listen for God's voice and watch for His directing. Many times waiting is our friend. God is a God of timing, and He is not bound by time and space. We are the one that has the boundaries and limitations. Never think: *"I don't have enough time."* We have all the time that God has allotted us, and that is enough.

Missionary Lottie Moon has been quoted as saying: *"You are invincible while doing the will of God for you."*

The hindrance could be: Wrong place or wrong time and even not God's will at all.

Think about it. *Selah!*

Day 3: Jesus Loves Me

"See what kind of love the Father has given to us that we should be called children of God; and so we are. The reason why the world does not know us is that it did not know him." **1 John 3:1 ESV**

I would venture to say that every person in these United States of America and Christians all around this world know the song, *"Jesus Loves Me."* We know those three words but the next three words we struggle with: *"This I know."* We are humbled to hear that Jesus loves us, but many times we struggle with the thought because we know ourselves so well and, therefore, are not always convinced of its dimensions. What is the width and height of his love and the volume of His love?

Why would He love us? We are not always convinced of the "this I know" because we know ourselves better than we know "Jesus loves me." We are quick to misplace the fact that "Jesus loves me" because of our own inability to love as He loves: completely, continually, and without condition.

There is but one way to really come to grips with the "FACT" that "Jesus loves me" and that is to accept and believe the next six words of the song: *"for the Bible tells me so."* We can be sure because His Word says so. Jesus said that He is the TRUTH, so do we believe Jesus? *"God is not man, that he should lie,"* **Numbers 23:19 ESV** tells us. So, do you believe Him?

These twelve words, "Jesus loves me this I know for the Bible tells me so," have defeated Satan, the liar and murderer (**John 8:44**), and satisfied the wrath of God for sin completely (**Hebrews 10:12**). He gave us His righteousness (**2 Corinthians 5:21**). Why did He do it? Because He wanted to do it, and that is reason enough. He honestly wants to love me.

Jesus doesn't love me because I am good, because there is none that is good, **Psalm 14:3.** His Word says, *"No one is good except God alone,"* **Mark 10:18 ESV.**

Jesus did not die for me because I was godly, but because I was ungodly. **Romans 5:6**

Jesus doesn't love me because I'm a Christian, because while I was still lost in my sin, Jesus died for me. **Romans 5:8**

Jesus doesn't love me because my dad and mother brought me up in the church, or because my dad was a preacher, or because I was born in a Christian nation. **2 Corinthians 5:10**

Jesus loves me because He wants to and because of His great love. I was given His righteousness in exchange for my sin, and He made me all new, **2 Corinthians 5:21.** I am all His work, all His doing, and compete in Him, **Ephesians 2:8-10.** The Bible tells me so! "Yes, Jesus loves me, the Bible tells me so!" I choose to believe it because Jesus said so.

Did you know that He loves you too? He asked me to tell you about it for Him. This is His Good News. Have you heard about it? He explains it in **John 3:16**. Check it out!

Think about it. *Selah!*

Day 4: What Is Easier?

"For which is easier, to say, 'Your sins are forgiven,' or to say, 'Rise and walk'?
Matthew 9:5 ESV

Did Jesus come to heal our bodies or to give us new bodies? Did Jesus come to make us rich or to give us His riches? Did Jesus come to make life free from trouble or to give us peace in the time of trouble? Did Jesus come to make us renowned and well known to the world or to make His name known in the world?

Ravi Zacharias has made the observation: *"Jesus didn't come to make bad people good, he came to make dead people alive,"* **Isaiah 53:5 ESV.** Here is the bottom line: Jesus came to do an impossible thing, a God thing, and something that no human or spirit could do. What He came to do was way beyond the capabilities of anyone or anything. If it is something that can be accomplished by human means, it's not a God thing.

In **Matthew 9:5** we have Jesus making this point to the people: Which is easier, to heal someone of a disease or to really forgive someone's sins? *"To forgive is divine,"* the poet Alexander Pope has written.

People can make other people rich and give all types of valuables to them, but God gives us His riches in heaven. We are admonished not to make our aim to have treasures on earth but to make our aim to have treasures in heaven, **Matthew 6:19-20**.

Jesus didn't come to set up a kingdom on earth but to tell us of His Kingdom. Satan did not understand this when he tempted Jesus. When he took Jesus on the high mountain and showed Him all the kingdoms, he said he would give them to Jesus if He would just worship him. Jesus said that God only is to be worshiped, **Matthew 4:10**.

Over emphasis on health, wealth, power or anything else can become worship, and Jesus is the only one worthy of our worship. Jesus didn't come to bring bread on earth, though He did provide bread, but He wanted us to see Him as the bread of life. He didn't come to do great things, although He did great things, but He came to do the great work of the Father and make us acceptable to the Father. He didn't come to clean up the earth but to tell us of the new earth that was to come.

By His stripes we have been healed of our sin and made clean and free of the penalty of sin. He took that punishment. He came to drink the whole cup of the gall of sin (**Matthew 26:39**) and left the sweet aroma of Christ in us (**2 Corinthians 2:15-16**).

Think about it. *Selah!*

Day 5: Does God Ever Change His Mind?

"No, I tell you; but unless you repent, you will all likewise perish." **Luke 13:3**

Does God ever change His mind? No. Does God ever relent? No. Yet, God does say that if we will obey (make a choice to turn from our sin), we will escape His pending judgment. Who changed? We did. Who repented or made a turn around? We did. God does warn of pending judgment. This is what the whole Gospel is about: forgiveness for sin and the command to repent or else.

Because God withdraws His hand does not mean that He has changed, it means He withdrew His hand of wrath because we have changed and repented.

God is faithful to His word and we are not.

James tells us to draw near to God and He will draw near to us. He tells us to resist the devil and he will flee. He flees because we are changing direction and going to God. When we make the right choice, we receive the blessing because we have changed from our wickedness and sin.

"If my people who are called by my name humble themselves, and pray and seek my face and turn from their wicked ways, then I will hear from heaven and will forgive their sin and heal their land." **2 Chronicles 7:14 ESV**

God does not change His mind. There is no shadow of turning in Him. *"Every good gift and every perfect gift is from above, coming down from the Father of lights with whom there is no variation or shadow due to change."* **James 1:17 ESV**

God is long suffering, patient and will do everything necessary to give the chance to change, repent, and turn from sin. **2 Peter 3:9**

Think about it. *Selah!*

Day 6: Boldly Come

"Therefore, brethren, having boldness to enter the Holiest by the blood of Jesus, by a new and living way which He consecrated for us, through the veil, that is, His flesh, and having a High Priest over the house of God, let us draw near with a true heart in full assurance of faith, having our hearts sprinkled from an evil conscience and our bodies washed with pure water. Let us hold fast the confession of our hope without wavering, for He who promised is faithful." **Hebrews 10:19-23 NKJV**

The "Holiest" of places: Would you feel comfortable going into your neighbor's house without knocking? How about the home of a sports celebrity, would you feel comfortable being there? Would it be possible to enter the White House unannounced without any fear or second thought? No, I would not feel comfortable or welcome in doing any of those things.

I remember seeing a picture of President John F. Kennedy talking on the phone in his office and John and Carolyn playing under the desk while all this was happening. How can they do that? They can do that boldly because the President was their daddy. They didn't have to knock before entering. They had no second thought about entering that room and asking the President to get them a drink out of the refrigerator or to go outside and play with them. He was their daddy. They were not being bold. They were confident and comfortable. It was second nature to them.

That is the way we can enter the very throne of God, the most Holy of all holy places. We can do this because we have the blood of Jesus and His righteousness upon us. He wants us to come, He asks us to come, and He wants to have fellowship with us because we are His children.

Coleman, who is 8 years old, and Nash, who is 5 years old, are two of my eight grandchildren. They have asked about a shotgun that I have. They want to shoot it. I told them that they were not old enough to shoot it, but when they get to be about 10 years old I would let them shoot it. I added to their request by saying, "And if your daddy and mother are willing, I will give you the shotgun to keep." They were okay with that answer but continued to ask me, "When will we be old enough?" The answer would always be, "When you turn 10." Their repeated requests do not bother me. I love it.

What about you? Do you hesitate about talking with God? Do you feel your request or need will go unheeded, unanswered, or unacknowledged by God? Well, He already knows your need and your request, and He is making arrangements. If it isn't today, it will be soon; and if not soon, there is something about that request that may harm us.

God wants to hear your voice. He loves to see you coming to His throne, and with eagerness, He has planned out just how He is going to respond to you. Oh, yes, He has plans for you, and His plans are for your good, not for your harm. **Jeremiah 29:11 ESV** says, *"For I know the plans I have for you, declares the Lord,* *plans for welfare and not for evil, to give you a future and a hope."*

One more thing, not only does the Father want us to come to Him, but Jesus and the Holy Spirit are there interceding for us.

Think about it. *Selah!*

Day 7: Live For Christ

"I have been crucified with Christ. It is no longer I who live, but Christ who lives in me. And the life I now live in the flesh I live by faith in the Son of God, who loved me and gave himself for me". **Galatians 2:20 ESV**

In the world in which we live, we often see and hear of men, women, and children who seek opportunities to die for their god. They do this because of the hope that they might gain the recognition of their god where he would allow them entrance to his heaven. "Allah is great," the Muslim believer proclaims; but is it great to require you to die for him in order to gain his favor?

The god of Islam proclaims that his followers must die for him. In stark contrast, Jehovah God sent his only Son, Jesus, to die for mankind that he might live. *"For God so loved the world that He gave His only begotten Son, that whosoever believes in Him should not perish but have everlasting life."* **John 3:16 NKJV**

God's aim is life not death. Believers have been killed, are being killed, and will be killed because of their Faith, but we are not called to die for Christ. He died for us. We do not try to exterminate others but seek to share our life and Faith with others. *". . . just as Christ was raised from the dead by the glory of the Father, we too might walk in newness of life."* **Romans 6:4 ESV**

What God wants is commitment to Him in spreading the Good News to others, and in our commitment, He will supply all we need as we spread the Good News. *". . . And the life I now live in the flesh I live by faith in the Son of God, who loved me and gave himself for me."* **Galatians 2:20 ESV**

Think about it. *Selah!*

Day 8: The Ungodly

"For while we were still weak, at the right time Christ died for the ungodly."
Romans 5:6 ESV

Have you fallen in your Christian life? Do you feel that there is no more hope for you? Do you feel that you are just too ungodly for God to care about you at all?

Well, I can say this with 100% confidence that you are 100% wrong! By the way, you were born into sin; you didn't grow into sin. Sin is your nature. You are the very person that Jesus came into this world for in the first place. Jesus came to redeem, not to accuse. Jesus is the Redeemer (*". . . who gave himself for us to redeem us. . ."* **Titus 2:14 ESV**) and Satan is the accuser (. . . *who accuses them day and night before our God"* **Revelation 12:10 ESV**).

No matter how far you may have fallen from the Lord, you never fall beyond God's forgiving heart. If God could save and use Paul, the chief of sinners (**I Timothy 1:15**), certainly He can save you too. Not only can He save, but He can save to the uttermost (**Hebrews 7:25:** *"Consequently, he is able to save to the uttermost those who draw near to God through him, since he always lives to make intercession for them"*). This is in reference to you, to you in particular.

"When we were utterly helpless, Christ came at just the right time and died for us sinners. Now most people

would not be willing to die for an upright person, though someone might perhaps be willing to die for a person who is especially good. But God showed his great love for us by sending Christ to die for us while we were still sinners."
Romans 5:6-8 NLT

Think about it. *Selah!*

Day 9: Misleading

". . . How could the two of you even think of conspiring to test the Spirit of the Lord like this?" **Acts 5:9 NLT**

Remember the account of Ananias and Sapphira in **Acts 5**? The lives of the couple were taken for lying to the Holy Spirit of God. What were they thinking? They thought they could fool God. It was Ananias who did the act and Sapphira knew about it and "connived" with him, as **The Message** paraphrases.

The scripture tells us that they "secretly" kept back a portion while misleading the rest of the church that they had given all. They lied to the Holy Spirit and announced openly that they were giving all. "Secretly" implies a carefully thought out plan.

I wonder if we find ourselves doing this today as we tithe? We rationalize that tithing is really not necessary or that it is less than we know it to be. We hold back portions for all types of reasons.

Tithing is an important part of the life of the believer because it is by tithing that we are able to experience an awesome display of blessing on our lives.

So, what am I saying? I'm saying that you cannot fool God, so obey God. I'm saying don't try to mislead other believers to think you are doing what you say you are doing. You may fool others but you cannot fool God. Be faithful, be obedient, and be honest.
Think about it. *Selah!*

Day 10: Peculiar

"Who gave himself for us, that he might redeem us from all iniquity, and purify unto himself a peculiar people, zealous of good works." **Titus 2:14 KJV**

Do you like to be called peculiar? To be peculiar is to be odd, strange, unusual, weird, eccentric, bizarre, or far-out. Peculiar is to be individual, distinctive representative, personal, and special. A peculiar person is not your normal, run-of-the-mill, everyday, and familiar person. There is something that is different about the person, and the difference makes that person peculiar.

The normal person cannot understand the peculiar person because they act differently and react differently from the normal. To be called peculiar can bring about a feeling of offense. But the King James Bible uses the word "peculiar" to describe the design of Jesus Christ for His people. He makes us peculiar and different, and we are different because we have been made righteous by God. Everyone else, the normal people, are still unrighteous; so, to the normal people of this world, we actually are peculiar. We are far-out man! Totally out of it! Out of this world all the way to the new world that Jesus is making for His peculiar people.

We are not of this world. We are peculiar, and we are of a heavenly one. The everyday people hate us because they hated Jesus. We are peculiar! Peculiar and proud of it! We are blessed because of it and set-apart from everyone else—we are peculiar. The peculiar people are "zealous" to do good works for the one who has made us peculiar.

Eugene Peterson paraphrases **Titus 2:14** this way: *"He offered himself as a sacrifice to free us from a dark, rebellious life into this good, pure life, making us a people he can be proud of, energetic in goodness,"* **The Message.** That is not the normal. It is peculiar to the world. The **New Living Translation** puts the verse this way: *"... to make us his very own people."* That is peculiar; we are peculiar and ought to be proud to be called special. Only set apart people will enter heaven.

Think about it. *Selah!*

Day 11: What Is It That People Expect To See?

"You will recognize them by their fruits." **Matthew 7:16 ESV**

Francis Chan in his book: <u>Forgotten God,</u> gives this illustration: *"If I told you I had an encounter with God where He entered my body and gave me a supernatural ability to play basketball, wouldn't you expect to see an amazing improvement in my jump shot, my defense, and my speed on the court? After all, this is God we're talking about. And if you saw no change in my athleticism, wouldn't you question the validity of my 'encounter'?*

Churchgoers all across the nation say the Holy Spirit has entered them. They claim that God has given them a supernatural ability to follow Christ, . . . Yet when those outside the church see no difference in our lives, they begin to question our integrity, our sanity, or even worse, our God. And can you blame them?"

What a troubling thought. So, what is it that the world expects to see in the genuine follower of Jesus Christ? Do they expect a churchgoer, a Sunday school teacher, a deacon, or a preacher? Not all who call me Lord will enter the Kingdom of Heaven, Jesus tells us (**Matthew 7:21**). Maybe they expect to see riches on earth, or healthy and healed people? None of these things mark a person as a follower of Jesus Christ.

Jesus tells us that we will know them by their fruit (**Matthew 7:20 KJV**). By their fruit you will know them, so, what are the fruits? Paul talks about the fruit of the Spirit in **Galatians 5:22-23 ESV:** *" But the fruit of the Spirit is love, joy, peace, patience, kindness, goodness, faithfulness, gentleness, self-control; . . . ."*

Love: *"By this all will know that you are My disciples, if you have love for one another."* **John 13:35 NKJV**

Joy: *"These things have I spoken to you that My joy may remain in you, and that your joy may be full."* **John 15:11 NKJV**

Peace: *"Peace I leave with you, . . . not as the world gives . . . ."* **John 14:27 NKJV**

Patience: Tribulation works patience. **Romans 5:3 KJV**

Kindness: The kindness of God leads to repentance. **Romans 2:4 ESV**

Goodness: *"Do not be overcome by evil, but overcome evil with good."* **Romans 12:21 ESV**

Faithfulness: *"If possible, so far as it depends on you, live peaceably with all."* **Romans 12:18 ESV**

Gentleness: *"Pursue righteousness, godliness, faith, love, steadfastness, gentleness."* **1 Timothy 6:11 ESV**

Self-Control: *"Add to your virtue self-control."* **2 Peter 1:6**

I'm thinking that if God says we should seek the fruit of the Spirit, then that is what people are looking for in us. Seek the Fruit. Show your Fruit.

Think about it. *Selah!*

Day 12: God Wants To Talk With You

"Come now, let us reason together, says the Lord:"
Isaiah 1:18 ESV

"But the Lord God called to the man and said to him, 'Where are you?' "
Genesis 3:9 ESV

It was a special time that God had with Adam and Eve. It was an appointed time that He had set to come and spend time with them. It had become a special time, a custom time, a habit, and an appointed time that He selected to come and spend with them. But this day, something was different. It was out of their normal schedule of the day. God had come down as usual, but His creation was not there. Something had happened and that something was disobedience. That disobedience caused an interruption in the relationship with mankind and God. That disobedience is sin, and sin continues to be the separation between God and mankind today.

Paul in **Romans 5:19 ESV** writes of this event: *"For as by the one man's disobedience the many were made sinners, so by the one man's obedience the many will be made righteous."*

Hebrews 4:15-16 ESV: *"For we do not have a high priest who is unable to sympathize without weaknesses, but one who in every respect has been tempted as we are, yet without sin. Let us then with confidence draw near to the throne of grace, that we may receive mercy and find*

grace to help in time of need."

Adam and Eve were not able to have confidence to come before their God and speak with Him because of their disobedience and sin. Now Jesus has corrected that situation and torn down that barrier, that separation that existed between God and His creation. We now have that freedom to come.

Though the barrier has been taken away, we often erect our own barrier, and still hide from God. We need to remember this:

1. God wants to talk to you.
2. He asks that you come alone to Him.
3. He wants to disclose to you that He knows what you actually need.
4. He wants to speak to you personally.
5. He wants to walk with you by yourself, just you and Him.
6. He wants to speak to you specifically.
7. He has offered you a personal invitation. RSVP

Is there a barrier in your life? God didn't put it there; He tore it down. So, where are you? That's God calling out to you.

Think about it. *Selah!*

Day 13: In The World But Not Of The World

"I do not ask that you take them out of the world, but that you keep them from the evil one. They are not of the world, just as I am not of the world. Sanctify them in the truth; your word is truth. As you sent me into the world, so I have sent them into the world." **John 17:15-18 ESV**

What is the mission of the believer today? Is it not to go into the world and make disciples? How do we accomplish this? We accomplish our commission by venturing out into this wicked world, among its wicked people and in the midst of its wicked environment, and telling them of the Good News, holding up its shining light, preserving them with the salt of mercy and grace, and living before them the sufficiency of life that is ours in Christ Jesus. We offer to them hope and life, eternal life in exchange for eternal death. We give them the bread of life in this barren land.   We are on a rescue mission, a "SEALS TEAM SIX" mission.

Here's the thing: we can't do this by separating ourselves from the world. We shouldn't expect to find Godly values in a world that is run by principalities and powers and workers of inequity in high and heavenly places.   We can only be successful in our disciple-making mission by engaging people where they are.

So, have your armor on, expect war, expect wickedness, expect hate, expect opposition, and unleash love. Spray our whole world with the love of God, the water of life, the light of Christ, and the preserving salt of the world, and watch God do what He does by His

Holy Spirit. The Holy Spirit is the one Who draws, Who convicts and Who points them to Jesus. We are His ambassadors.

Here's the deal: Go out into the world; don't stay in the church. Don't seek retreats. We are not supposed to retreat. We need to stand in the power of God's might. Look for opportunities to tell the Good News and watch God work.

Think about it. *Selah!*

Day 14: What Can I Do?

"For if you remain completely silent at this time, relief and deliverance will arise for the Jews from another place, but you and your father's house will perish. Yet who knows whether you have come to the kingdom for such a time as this."
Esther 4:14 NKJV

We do live in a very difficult world today, but to be honest, it has always been a difficult world in which to live. But you can be sure, this world is not getting better; it is getting worse. Sin is rampant and Christians are being persecuted and killed just because they are Christians and no one seems to have a passion to do anything about it. Perhaps we have the feeling that there is really nothing that one person can do.

Queen Esther felt this way in her time when the Jews were being persecuted for being Jews. Her cousin, Mordecai who had raised her after her mother and father had died, challenged her to do something about the situation because of the position that she was in. But Esther did not feel that she was capable of doing anything. She was just one person. Mordecai reminded her that she was where she was just for this very moment. He didn't want her to miss her opportunity. They say, "Opportunity only knocks once," and it is true. Mordecai's challenge was this: *"Yet who knows whether you have come to the kingdom for such a time as this."*
Esther 4:14 NKJV

This is a question that we all should ask ourselves as

well.   Perhaps I have been placed here for this very moment to make a difference. Yet you may think, *"But I'm only one person."* You would be right, but it only takes one to turn the tide. It is not just you; it is you and God.

Let me ask another question, what would you do for the Lord Jesus Christ if you knew for certain that you would not fail? Now, if you feel strongly about your calling and you understand *"I can do all things through Christ Jesus my Lord"* (Philippians 4:13) and that *"my God shall supply all my need according to his riches in heaven through Christ Jesus"* (Philippians 4:19), and you believe that *"He who began a good work in you will be faithful to complete it"* (Philippians 1:6), and that *"He is able to do exceedingly abundantly above all that you ask or think"* (Ephesians 3:20), and understand that, *"with God all things are possible"* (Matthew 19:26), then Jesus would say to you what He told His disciples while on the boat in a storm on the Sea of Galilee*: "Where is your faith?"* Luke 8:25

Now, why don't you do what you feel you should do? You can succeed. Things haven't really changed. It was hard for Esther to live among the Medes and Persians. They crucified Christ in Jerusalem. They martyred the early church leaders and still Christians are martyred today. Don't fear those who kill the body but he who can destroy the soul (Matthew 10:28).

For This Very Hour

In this land of milk and honey,
With God's blessing rich and free,
Sin still reigns and seems to flourish,
Who will stand, my servant be?

Just consider, God in wisdom,
Formed, equipped with His great power,
And has placed me in this country,
For this time, this very hour.

Ripened harvest, needing laborers,
Will you now my servant be?
I'm unworthy, Lord to serve you,
Naught have I to give to Thee.

Just consider, God in wisdom,
Formed, equipped with His great power,
And has placed me in this country,
For this time, this very hour.

Lord, I stand an empty vessel,
Empty, open Lord to Thee.
Lead me Lord and I will follow,
When and where You may lead me.

Just consider, God in wisdom,
Formed, equipped with His great power,
And has placed me in this country,
For this time, this very hour.

Danny G. Thomas

God is not calling you to do what you are capable of doing but, rather, He is calling you to do what He is capable of doing through you at this very moment and in this very hour.

Think about it. *Selah!*

Day 15: This Little Light Of Mine

"Nor do people light a lamp and put it under a basket, but on a stand, and it gives light to all in the house."
Matthew 5:15 ESV

> *"This little light of mine, I'm gonna' let it shine,*
> *This little light of mine, I'm gonna' let it shine,*
> *Let it shine, let it shine, let it shine."*

Most likely, you have sung this chorus as a child. We had it sung to us by our parents perhaps even before we could speak. Light cannot be hidden unless we choose to hide it and make provisions. Light destroys darkness. Where there is light, there cannot be darkness at all. Even a small candle can be seen for miles on a dark night.

Jesus uses light as an example of our life and our message to the world. We should not do anything to hide our light. We should lift up our light. Light attracts attention in darkness. Light reveals what is true or trusting and what is false, dangerous, or destructive. Light is a necessity to be able to move about with confidence, to get around without fear, and to give understanding.

Jesus is The Light of the world and we are the light holder, the candle stand upon which The Light is held. The only thing needed is for the candle stand to be available to have The Light placed upon it. The stand does not have to be ornate and it does not have to have value. It merely needs to be used. A little wax placed upon a surface will secure a candle. Are you available? No one will notice a holder unless there is a lit candle upon it. You may even have a candle in the stand but if it is not lit, what is noticed is the stand, and the stand has no purpose of true value.

What I am saying is, let Jesus use you; let Him shine to those around you. That little light that you have . . . let it shine.

Think about it. *Selah!*

Day 16: Holy Eyes

"For in him all the fullness of God was pleased to dwell, and through him to reconcile to himself all things, whether on earth or in heaven, making peace by the blood of his cross. And you, who once were alienated and hostile in mind, doing evil deeds, he has now reconciled in his body of flesh by his death, in order to present you holy and blameless and above reproach before him."
Colossians 1:20-22 ESV

Have you ever considered the eyes of God? God is holy and He cannot look upon unholiness or unrighteousness without unleashing His wrath. Unholiness and unrighteousness deserve and summon the wrath of a holy God. So, how can a Holy God look upon the Christian with approval? Something has to change in order for God to reconcile, or to appease His holy eyes or to make the needed atonement for His wrath.

Jesus is the answer here. It is Jesus who took our unrighteousness and exchanged it for His own righteousness (**2 Corinthians 5:21**). When Jesus died upon the cross, our sins were nailed there with Him (**Colossians 2:14**). At that very moment the pure blood of Jesus made a complete atonement, a pure sacrifice for our sin (**Hebrews 10:11-12**).

Because of that sacrifice, that atonement for sin, the debt of our sin was satisfied and we were made pure, clean, and holy in the sight of God the Father. As He looks upon us, He sees His righteous, clean, and holy son. We have become a child of God. How awesome is that?

It is not goodness that makes us clean, for the very best of the best of mankind's righteousness is sickening, filthy rags in the holy eyes of God. Yes, by being placed in Christ and having His righteousness placed upon us, we are now viewed by the Father as unstained and unmarked by sin. All our sins have been forgiven, just as though we had never sinned at all. We are made holy, just for the holy eyes of the Father.

Holy Eyes

If we come to the Father with confession of sin,
God is faithful and just, He will forgive us and then,
He will cleanse us in purity, as though we had not sinned.

And He views us with holy eyes,
Unstained, unmarked by sin.
All our sins in Him forgiven
Just as though they had not been.

Oh, 'tis good just to know we have a Savior in Christ,
Who was sent by His Father as a final sacrifice.
'Twas His gift to redeem mankind from darkness into light.
And He views us with holy eyes,
Unstained, unmarked by sin.
All our sins in Him forgiven
Just as though they had not been.

I sing praise to the Father; He's the giver of life,
Who has power to free us from this sin and anguished
strife,
But our faith must be kept in Him to have eternal life.

And He views us with holy eyes,
Unstained, unmarked by sin.
All our sins in Him forgiven
Just as though they had not been.

We can trust in Him completely; what He says He will
do.
He'll give power to conquer sin; no temptation's new.
But will with the temptation, an escape will come in
view.

And He views us with holy eyes,
Unstained, unmarked by sin.
All our sins in Him forgiven
Just as though they had not been.

Danny G. Thomas

Think about it. *Selah!*

Day 17: Why Study?

"Study to show thyself approved unto God, a workman that needeth not to be ashamed, rightly dividing the word of truth." **2 Timothy 2:15 KJV**

Study: My dad frequently would repeat this little statement to remind me that at times people may tell me something that sounds reasonable and right, but actually it is far from the truth. He instilled into me a wall of protection, a defense mechanism that would help me determine real truth. The little phrase went like this:

> *The more you study, the more you know,*
> *The more you know the more you forget,*
> *The more you forget the less you know.*
>
> *The less you study the less you know,*
> *The less you know, the less you forget,*
> *The less you forget, the more you know,*
> *So, why study!*

Though it may sound reasonable, it is totally wrong. To study is to know and you cannot know unless you study. Someone has said, *"There is a huge gap between being exactly right and almost right."* To be almost right is to be totally wrong. Things are either right or they are wrong, and there is no gray area between the two. And it you have the knowledge and do not accurately relay it, you are a deceiver or liar.

Paul wanted Timothy to know the value of studying.

Studying makes one wise, it makes one informed, and it gives credibility to what one believes. The caution in studying is making sure that you get the right information and being able to apply the right information in the right situation.

I'm sure you have heard this statement: *"Practice makes perfect."* Well, that is a lie. Actually *"Practice makes permanent."* If you practice incorrectly, then you are incorrect. You think you are correct but you are wrong; you are imperfect. If your practice is correct, then you are right on the road to perfection. Practice makes permanent.

A student of the Word of God has a goal to rightly divide the Word of Truth. The **New Living Translation** relays **2 Timothy 2:15** like this: *"Work hard so you can present yourself to God and receive his approval. Be a good worker, one who does not need to be ashamed and who correctly explains the word of truth."*

A.W. Tozer has written: *"The task of the scholar is to guarantee the purity of the text, to get as close as possible to the Word as originally given. He may compare Scripture with Scripture until he discovers the true meaning of the text, but right there his authority ends. He must never sin in judgment upon what is written. He must not bring the meaning of the Word before the bar of reason."*

One last thought, there is no opinion in truth. There is no debate in truth. Truth is the truth; it is the whole truth and contains nothing but the truth. Dr. Michael

Catt, our pastor at Sherwood Baptist Church, is fond of quoting Evangelist Ron Dunn and one of those quotes is: *"May I tell you in my humble and inaccurate opinion, which I highly respect."* Don't put too much credence in your opinion, stick to the facts, and stick to the truth and nothing but the truth. Never come to the point where you feel you have all of the answers. You need to study, and the more you study, you will find that you need to study all the more. So, *"Why study?"*—to find the truth.

Study to show thyself approved.

Think about it. *Selah!*

Day 18: Reasoning With God

"Come now, let us reason together, says the Lord: though your sins are like scarlet, they shall be as white as snow; though they are red like crimson, they shall become like wool. If you are willing and obedient, you shall eat the good of the land; but if you refuse and rebel, you shall be eaten by the sword." **Isaiah 1:18-20 ESV**

To reason with God, what is that like? The *New Living Translation* renders reason: *Argue this out.* But to argue with God should be to find out the truth, not to be stubborn and rebellious because then there is no hope for discovering the truth. To reason with God is to enter into divine knowledge and understanding and to depart from human reasoning.

In **Romans 12:2,** Paul tells the church at Rome not to be conformed to this present world's way of thinking and reasoning. Worldly thought processes, mindsets, and reasoning change as time goes on. The "right way" to act in one generation is always open to challenge by the next generation. What once was considered right and reasonable at one time is rejected by the next generation.

God's reasoning is always the same. His reasoning never changes: *"Jesus Christ the same, yesterday, today and forever,"* **Hebrews 13:8 NKJV.** God is all knowing. There is nothing that He does not know, and there was never a time in which He didn't know all that there is to know. There will never be a time that He will not know all that there is to know. That is mind boggling to humanity.

Paul continues on in **Romans 12:2** by saying that we need to be transformed by the renewing of our minds. We need to be reprogrammed with new software, and that is divine knowledge, understanding, and wisdom.

In short, our mind is not anything near to God's mind, therefore, we need to accept what He says as truth and accept it by faith because we are incapable of understanding it. So when we come to the Lord for reasoning, we should just obey what He says and not give in to our natural inclination of rebellion against His reasoning.

The only way to prove what is the good and acceptable will of God is by the renewing or reprogramming of our mind.

Think about it. *Selah!*

Day 19: Earnest And Sincere Prayer

"So Peter was kept in prison, but earnest prayer for him was made to God by the church." **Acts 12:5 ESV**

To do something in earnest is to do it in faith toward something; it is to do it constantly and fervently. It is done in sincerity, or with the whole heart, and is done in good faith. In **Acts 12** we find the church experiencing the death of one Apostle, James, his brother Peter being placed in prison, and their own fate being at great risk. The fledgling, young, and now struggling church found itself being challenged by the government and the religious leaders of the day. They were at risk of death themselves. What were they to do? Their natural response was prayer and that is what they earnestly did. They prayed sincerely for the saving of Peter from the grip of those in authority.

Did they believe in prayer? Yes, they did. Did they expect an answer to their prayer? Yes, they did, but still they needed help with their unbelief. Remember the event of a father bringing his demon-possessed boy to Jesus in **Mark 9**? The very action of the father to bring his child to Jesus expressed belief in Jesus, but he still added the phrase *"if you can"* to his request of help from Jesus. There was a bit of unbelief or doubt in the heart of the father. Jesus drew attention to that phrase and said, *"If I can?"* He then asked the father if he believed that He was able to help his son, and the father responded, *"Yes, I believe but help my unbelief."* That was what was happening to the church here in Acts, and we also experience a bit of unbelief as we *"earnestly"*

pray.

That little bit of doubt and unbelief caused unnecessary pain and grief to them. When we pray, we need to pray with expectation of an answer and leave it with God. Our spirit is willing to believe but our body is weak in believing (**Mark 14:38**). Remember, God is not bound by time but timing means everything to God. Timing is of utmost importance. Timing is *"in the fullness of time."* It is *"the right time"* and that is the time God sends His answer.

Now that leads me to you. What is it that you are praying to God for an answer? Do you believe? I feel certain that you do believe, just by the mere fact that you have been praying and are continuing to pray. I would encourage you to keep on praying, keep on believing, and you will get the answer to your prayer. When you get the answer, obey what God reveals to you, and you will experience that peace of God that passes all understanding. You will receive the added strength of God's joy in your life. Not only will you receive that peace and joy but it will strengthen your hope for the future as it will all those around you as well.

Think about it. *Selah!*

Day 20: I'm Forgiven?

"If we confess our sins, he is faithful and just to forgive us our sins and to cleanse us from all unrighteousness.." **1 John 1:9 ESV**

As Jesus communed with his disciples in the upper room, He gave them an object lesson and He asked that they rehearse that lesson frequently for the rest of their lives. We refer to that lesson as the Lord's Supper or Communion. As often as you do this, do it in remembrance of me, He said. And today each time we observe the Lord's Supper or we take Communion, once again it causes us to think about and to remember the sacrifice of Jesus for us.

Forgiven! When we repent of our sins to God and accept Jesus' gift of righteousness, we are free of the penalty of sin. Our sins have been totally and completely forgiven and forgotten by the Father. Think about that for a moment; for God to forget is the greatest miracle of all! He who is all knowing, chooses to remove some of that knowledge and remember it no more, forever!

The whole Trinity is involved in this miracle of forgiveness and forgetting. The Father is the one who can forgive sin, the Son is the reason the Father can forgive, and the Holy Spirit is the guarantee to us that He has forgiven us and forgotten our sin.

Although we may not forget our sins, and perhaps we may not forgive ourselves of our sins, God has and He can be trusted. He blots them out, totally, and has cast them in the great sea of His forgetfulness as far as the east is from the west. It is now as though they had never been committed. We can stand clean, pure, and holy before God the Father, robed in the righteousness of Jesus.

Forgiveness is ours for the asking and with that forgiveness there is a guarantee that comes with it.

By the way, have you asked for forgiveness? If you have, then you are forgiven, totally!

Think about it. *Selah!*

Day 21: A False Balance

"A false balance is an abomination to the Lord, but a just weight is his delight. **Proverbs 11:1 ESV**

We're all saying the same thing; we all are going the same way. I hear that a lot when talking to people about God. All religions are the same, they say. We just need to learn to get along together and adjust our way of thinking.

How can you compare our God to a god? How can you adjust your thinking? There is and can only be one God supreme and any other god is merely something we highly treasure. A comparison of the two will only reveal the one that falls short of the standard.

If you are going to construct something, you must have a reliable ruler, square, and level. If any of those standards of measurement are untrue, the structure will be faulty, dangerous, and untrustworthy. The United States of America as well as other countries have standards of measurements. In the USA, the National Institute of Standards and Technology (NST), a division of the U. S. Department of Commerce, regulates the standards of measurements. These standards enable a comparison to be done between different measurements and reduce confusion.

If we are going to make a comparison of God and a god, we must have an unchanging standard of measurement that will eliminate confusion. God's Word never changes ("*All scripture is breathed out by God and*

profitable for teaching, for reproof, for correction, and for training in righteousness, that the man of God may be complete, equipped for every good work," **2 Timothy 3:16 ESV**). Jesus never changes (*"Jesus Christ the same yesterday, and today and forever,"* **Hebrews 13:8 KJV**).

God's credibility is based upon His word alone. Jesus is a tried and true cornerstone and can be trusted. Make God's Word your measure, make Jesus your foundation, and you will find you have a well built, wise, sure, and true life, and one that is well pleasing to God, confidently lived, and a benefit and blessing to all others.

Think about it. *Selah!*

Day 22: Winning

"I press toward the goal for the prize of the upward call of God in Christ Jesus." **Philippians 3:14 NKJV**

Vince Lombardi, the Hall of Fame football coach of the Green Bay Packers is quoted as saying: *"Winning is not a sometime thing, it's an all the time thing . . . You don't win once in a while, you don't do things right once in a while, you do them right all the time . . . Winning is a habit; unfortunately, so is losing."*

A winner is a worker. A winner is obedient to the fundamentals, those things that are at the foundation of a winner. Obedience to the Word of God is fundamental to victory in the life of a believer. It too, is not a once in a while thing. It is an all the time thing.

The Bible says that if we hide the Word of God in our heart (**Psalm 119:11**) and exercise it in our daily lives, it will become part of us, and then we will become real winners, all the time winners.

Think about it. *Selah!*

Day 23: Irritated

"Love is patient and kind. Love is not jealous or boastful or proud or rude. It does not demand its own way. It is not irritable, and it keeps no record of being wronged." **1 Corinthians 13:4-5 NLT**

Does it appear to you that people are becoming more and more irritated? Does it seem to you that you have become prone to finding failures and shortcoming in the lives of those people that you come in contact with in your every day schedule? I'm talking about that person ahead of you; you know, the one in your way. What are they thinking? Where were they raised anyway?

Wait a minute, could it be that perhaps it's not them but you who is the point of irritation? Could it be that you need to become more patient and kind? As I look at myself in the mirror, I believe I see some smudges, some dirty marks that have marred the image of Christ in my life.

"Or do you despise the riches of His goodness, forbearance, and longsuffering, not knowing that the goodness of God leads you to repentance?" **Romans 2:4 NKJV**

Think about it. *Selah!*

Day 24: As They Are

"Love . . . does not demand it's own way. Love . . . endures through every circumstance . . . . But love will last forever!" **1 Corinthians 13:5, 7-8 NLT**

My mother has said to me when I complained about someone: *"Danny, Jesus tells us we are to love others just as He loves the Father and others. If you're going to love people, you're going to have to love them as they are."*

That was not what I was wanting to hear. I wanted to hear, "You know, you're right. Those people need to be punished, they need to change!" Well, they may need punishment, and so do we. They may also need to change, but they won't change unless we love them and lead them to a better alternative.

Real love takes people where they are and encourages them by finding some good element in their life and expanding upon it to the point that it takes up more space in their lives and crowds out some of those bad characteristics. *"Stir up the gift that is in you,"* **2 Timothy 1:6.** They become impressed with you and begin to take on some of your good deeds, **2 Timothy 2:2.**

Rejoice with them in their progress, **1 Corinthians 13:6.** Focus on improvements, be patient, forget about failures, and resist comparing to others.

If you're going to love others as Christ loves you, then you must take them as they are, but don't leave them as they are. Display to them the love of God.

Think about it. *Selah!*

Day 25: "There He Misseth And Speaketh Without The Book"

"But Jesus told him, 'No! The Scriptures say, People do not live by bread alone, but by every word that comes from the mouth of God.'" Matthew **4:4 NLT**

Twenty-six year old Anne Askew, was tortured and burned at the stake in England as a heretic for her refusal to recant that the bread and wine taken in Communion had not been transformed into the actual body and blood of Jesus, called the doctrine of Transubstantiation. Just before she was burned, Bishop Shaxton questioned her: *"Thou foolish woman, sayest thou that priests cannot make the body of Christ?"* Her response was: *"I say so, my lord. I have read that God made man; but that man can make God, I never yet read, nor, I suppose, shall ever read; that which you call your God is a piece of bread; for proof thereof let it lie in a box three months, and it will be moldy."* Bishop Shaxton then began to preach and as Anne sat there chained to the post and in great pain from the rack, which had disjointed her ankles, knees, hips, shoulders and wrist, she would voice agreement with an "Amen!" when he spoke the truth; and when he didn't, she would loudly retort: *"There he misseth and speaketh without the Book!"* **(Fox's Book of Martyrs)**

My grandfather Thomas was a very plain spoken, bold, and brash man. He saw everything in black and white; there were no shady areas, especially when it came to Scripture. When he was in church listening to the preacher preach and quote a Scripture verse, if it was not quoted exactly as it was written in the King James Bible, my grandfather would loudly respond with: *"The Bible don't say that!"*

After my dad was ordained into the Gospel Ministry and my grandfather came to hear him preach, my dad told me that he was so apprehensive as he preached, fearing that if he accidentally misquoted a Scripture his dad would respond with: *"The Bible don't say that!"*

The Bible is so frequently misquoted and applied. If Scripture is misquoted or misapplied it is false. Satan quoted Scripture but misapplied it and the misapplication was a lie. May I challenge you to know Scripture and know how to apply it. The Holy Spirit is our teacher and if you need help, go to the teacher, the authority, the One that Jesus left for us for knowledge, wisdom, direction and comfort.

If you speak anything else: *"There you misseth and speaketh without the Book."*

Think about it. *Selah!*

Day 26: God's Will, How Do I Know?

"And do not be conformed to this world, but be transformed by the renewing of your mind, that you may prove what is that good and acceptable and perfect will of God." **Romans 12:2 NKJV**

Bobby Richardson, the Hall of Fame second baseman for the New York Yankees and evangelist, is noted as saying: *"God's will, nothing more, nothing less, nothing else."* What is God's Will? God's will is his personal plan for you and for your life. God's will is a personally divinely designed mission for you to live before others and to minister to others. God's will for you will allow you to successfully make a difference in the lives of others for the cause of Christ. *"For I know the plans I have for you, declares the Lord, plans for welfare and not for evil, to give you a future and a hope."* **Jeremiah 29:11 ESV**

To know God's will gives meaning to your life. It brings happiness to your life and gives hope. So, how does one discover the Will of God in his life? First, you cannot know it by employing earthly methods of determining what you are most suited for in life. It is by replacing those methods with seeking the leadership of the Holy Spirit and being sensitive to His leadership to that which He has fitted for you. It has nothing to do with what you are capable of doing, but what God is capable of doing through you.

One must develop a new way of thinking, a new way of doing, and that is God's way. It is a "wait and see"

way. **Isaiah 40:31** gives us the understanding that it is those who wait on the Lord that will do great things, unbelievable things, things that God has prepared for you to do. Therefore, if you want God's will, nothing more, nothing less, and nothing else, then you must transform your way of thinking and wait for God to move in your life and make His will known for your life.

Think about it. *Selah!*

Day 27: "How Much Praying Is Being Done By The Third Army?"

"Pray without ceasing." **1 Thessalonians 5:17 KJV**

It was December 8, 1944 at Caserne Molifor in Nancy, France, and the Third Army of General George Patton was bogged down in the rain-soaked soil and unable to move. General George Patton sent for his Senior Chaplin, James H. O'Neil and asked for *"a good prayer for good weather. Something must be done with this rain if we are going to win."* He asked the Chaplin, *"How much praying is being done by the Third Army?"* The Chief Chaplin O'Neil responded: *"Does the General mean by chaplains or by the men?"* *"By everybody,"* the General said. To this I countered by saying: *"I'm afraid to admit it, but I do not believe that much praying is going on. When there is fighting, everyone prays, but now with this constant rain – when things are quiet, dangerously quiet, men just sit and wait for things to happen. Prayer out there is difficult . . . I don't believe much praying is being done."*

Patton then said: *"Chaplin, I'm a strong believer in prayer. After you plan and prepare for battle, there is one other factor, the unknown; the unknown is where God moves, some may call it luck, I call it God's hand . . . Urge all of your men to pray, not alone in church, but everywhere. Pray when you are driving. Pray when fighting. Pray with others. Pray by night and pray by day. Pray for the cessation of immoderate rains, for good weather for Battle. Pray for the defeat of our wicked enemy whose banner is injustice and whose good is*

oppression. Pray for victory. Pray for our Army, and pray for peace."

A written prayer was sent out to all soldiers on the 12th through the 14th of December. What happened next was that the German Army could not fight because of the rain and fog and began to retreat and were bogged down and worn out by the weather. On December 20th, the skies cleared to find a beleaguered German Army vulnerable to the Allied planes and guns and the victory was realized.

"The things which are impossible with men are possible with God." **Luke 18:27 NKJV**

"Then He spoke a parable to them, that men always ought to pray and not lose heart," **Luke 18:1 NKJV**

"Pray without ceasing." **1 Thessalonians 5:17 KJV**

What are the unknowns in your life? How much praying is being done in your house?

Think about it. *Selah!*

Day 28: Beware Of Antichrist

"Dear children, the last hour is here. You have heard that the Antichrist is coming, and already many such antichrists have appeared. For this we know that the last hour has come." **1 John 2:18 NLT**

You can be certain of this fact: Anything or anyone who may promote division and hate is not of Christ; it is the spirit of antichrist. Any pastor, church leader, or Christian organization that breathes hate rather than love is against the Good News of Christ Jesus. If anyone says he is a Christian and hates and causes division, that person is a liar and not a believer. That person has the spirit of antichrist. **1 John 2:16-21**

If someone demands justice in the name of Christ, he is not a Christian. Anyone who promotes anything other than forgiveness, grace, and mercy is not of Christ. He is a liar and from such people turn away. If getting even or demanding rights are at the foremost of someone's purpose, it is not of God. Don't fall for it; run from it and warn other believers about it.

Jesus is the overcomer. He is the victor, and we are His followers, His messengers, and His ambassadors. Our message has everything to do about Him and carrying His message to them.

Think about it. *Selah!*

Day 29: So Hate Won't Win!

"I am writing these things to warn you about those who want to lead you astray. But you have received the Holy Spirit, and he lives within you, so you don't need anyone to teach you what is true." **1 John 2:26-27 NLT**

The cry of the follower of Jesus Christ in the very grip of injustice, hate, and persecution is not justice, for justice belongs to God alone. The cry is not for vengeance, for vengeance is mine says the Lord our God.

The message we carry is one of repentance, a turning around from the way of sin and the penalty of death to forgiveness and eternal life, which replaces our doom of eternal death. That message was so clearly and loudly proclaimed by the believers and family members of Mother Emmanuel AME Church in Charleston, South Carolina, at the setting of bail for the mass murderer Dylann Roof. Anthony Thompson, husband of Myra Thompson, one of the nine slaughtered at the prayer meeting that Wednesday night said, *"I forgive you and my family forgives you. But we would like for you to take this opportunity to repent and change your ways. Jesus Christ offers you forgiveness."*

Daniel Simmons' grandson proclaimed: *"A hateful person came to this community with some crazy idea he'd be able to divide, but all he did was unite us and make us love each other more. So hate won't win."*

There is an awesome peace that comes with forgiveness and love expressed from a loving heart. Only God can do that.

Think about it. *Selah!*

Day 30: He Will Keep You Strong

"He will keep you strong to the end so that you will be free from all blame on the day when our Lord Jesus Christ returns." **1 Corinthians 1:8 NLT**

Does it worry you about having the strength to remain true to Christ Jesus in this fearful time we are living in? Perhaps that is a concern that many followers of Jesus Christ have today. I feel that persecution and opposition to Christian believers will get greater and greater very quickly. So, we ask ourselves, will I stand strong? I believe this is not the question we must ask. The question is, Lord what would you have me do? When the believer is involved in doing what God has called him or her to do, it is God who provides the strength because we do His will in His power.

God does not call us to do what we can do; He calls us to do what He empowers us to do. He supplies all that is needed in our mission, right up to the very end. This is His promise, and so we ought not be concerned about strength. We move and have our being in Him.

Notice that **1 Corinthians 1:8** assures the believer of strength and freedom from blame also. There is no blame; there is strength to do, power to perform and assurance in knowing that we will do it right, without blame. For with God all things are possible. We can do all things through Christ Jesus our Lord.

Don't worry about strength and don't be concerned about endurance. For when you are in Him and in His strength and are clothed in His righteousness, you have all you need.

Think about it. *Selah!*

Day 31: Patience Personified

"The Lord is not slack concerning His promise, as some count slackness, but is longsuffering toward us, not willing that any should perish but that all should come to repentance." **2 Peter 3:9 NKJV**

Do you often find yourself irritated and angry at all the evil that is so evident and obvious to the eye today? Hate, mass murder, and slaughter at the hand of self-proclaimed executioners, who violently disagree with the mindset of Christians and peace-loving people, achieve their goal. There seems to be no champion to come to our defense. Does the question frequently pop-up in your mind, why? Why doesn't God do something about it? Why is it that good people get incurable, grievous, and debilitating diseases? Why is it that injustice seems to go unchallenged and unpunished for so long? And to these questions many more are added. Why?

Patience—it is tribulation that is needed to work out or bring about patience. Without tribulation there can be no patience and without patience nothing good can be accomplished.

Jonathan Edwards, the great revivalist, educator, philosopher, pastor, and missionary of the 1700's noted: *"There are the black clouds of God's wrath now hanging directly over your heads, full of the dreadful storm, and big with thunder, and were it not for the restraining hand of God* (patience) *it would immediately burst upon you. The sovereign pleasure of God, for the*

present, stays His rough wind; otherwise it would come in fury, and your destruction would come like a whirlwind, and you would be like the chaff of the summer threshing floor."

The Bible states it this way: *"The Lord is not slack concerning His promise, as some count slackness, but is longsuffering toward us, not willing that any should perish but that all should come to repentance,"* **2 Peter 3:9 NKJV.** Eugene Peterson paraphrases it this way in **The Message:** *"God isn't late with his promise as some measure lateness. He is restraining himself on account of you, holding back the End because he doesn't want anyone lost. He's giving everyone space and time to change."*

It is God's love that requires Him to bring a pause before His wrath. It is God's love that demands a peace before the storm of judgment, a time of waiting before the last sentence of life is written in His book. **Psalm 139:16** says: *"... And in your book they all were written. The days fashioned for me, When as yet there were none of them,"* **NKJV.** So, why? Because God wants to give everyone all the time necessary to allow people to repent of his or her sin. And we believers are God's ambassadors. We are the reflection of His patience, mercy, grace, and love in this pause. We display the hope and the peace that is sufficient in the struggle of life. We get diseases, we are falsely accused, and we experience the tragedy and the turmoil that are part of this world, which is controlled by its prince, Satan. This is not heaven nor is it hell, but God pauses in this wickedness, in this our hour, not wanting anyone to perish with this world.

We must trust God's patience and develop that divine patience, knowing that God is not unaware of what is happening. He knew about this very hour way before the creation of our world, and He made provision for it. He allowed enough time for each creation to repent, to change; but after this time comes the judgment. *"It is a fearful thing to fall into the hands of the living God,"* **Hebrews 10:31.**

So, believer, is there a struggle in your life? Trust God. He is aware of it, and He has prepared you for it. Be patient. *This too shall pass.* If you are one of those whom God is waiting on, one of those that He is *patiently* waiting upon, consider your ways, repent, and be saved. God is very long-suffering.

Think about it. *Selah!*

Day 32: Prepared For Worship

"So Moses went down from the mountain to the people and consecrated the people: and they washed their garments. And he said to the people, 'Be ready for the third day;' " **Exodus 19:14-15 ESV**

I remember Sunday mornings when I was growing up. They were different from all the other days of the week. We had to get ready for Sunday; we had to be prepared for that day. We had our baths on Saturday night, and as Sunday morning came, we put on our best clothes. My sisters wore a special dress, and my brother and I wore either a special shirt or a white shirt and tie. Our shoes were shined and our hair our special day of worship, and we had to be prepared.

Worship takes preparation. It doesn't just happen. Everyone must take steps of preparation. We need to come before the Lord with clean bodies, clean minds, and a clean spirit. If we come clean, sanctified, consecrated, and purified before a holy God, we will find him. Everything else must be left behind. We come "outside the camp," away from the normal to the divine, and we worship together, enjoying the presence of God. We love each other and we love God.

Do you come prepared for worship on Sundays? Or, do you come rushed, frustrated, aggravated, and with your mind on things other than a holy God. Notice what happened as the people came prepared outside the camp in **Exodus 19:17-20:** *"Moses led the people out of the camp to meet God. They stood at attention at the base*

of the mountain. Mount Sinai was all smoke because God had come down on it as fire. Smoke poured from it like smoke from a furnace. The whole mountain shuddered in huge spasms. The trumpet blasts grew louder and louder. Moses spoke and God answered in thunder. God descended to the peak of Mount Sinai. God called Moses up to the peak and Moses climbed up." **The Message**

The people came prepared and God came down. Do you come prepared for worship?

Think about it. *Selah!*

Day 33: What Is Life All About? What Is Its Purpose? I Wonder?

"But my life is worth nothing to me unless I use it for finishing the work assigned me by the Lord Jesus—the work of telling others the Good News about the wonderful grace of God." **Acts 20:24 NLT**

Do you ever wonder about your purpose? Does your life, at times, seem to be a great mystery? Do you ever wonder: *"Why am I here?"* I would say that most people have had that thought run through their minds on more than one occasion, and many dwell upon that thought. I wonder . . . what is life all about?

There are at least five questions that one must address in a quest to discover purpose in life:

1. I wonder, just who am I?
2. I wonder, why am I here?
3. I wonder, who is God?
4. I wonder, what is it that God would have me to do?
5. I have the Wonder of Wonders and I want you to discover Him too.

Paul, tells the believers at Ephesus, that *" . . . life is worth nothing to me unless I use it for finishing the work assigned me by the Lord Jesus—the work of telling others the Good News about the wonderful grace of God."* **Acts 20:24 NLT**

Paul knew his purpose and was ready for it, come what may. Paul was happy. He was engaged in doing his mission in life. Happiness is discovered when one discovers the plan that God has for him. The wonder in life is having the Wonder of Wonders and sharing it with a wondering world.

One of my favorite hymns is "The Wonder of It All," composed by George Beverly Shea, the famed soloist with the Billy Graham Evangelistic Association. He tells of a story behind the hymn: "*I was on the ocean liner S. S. United States in route to meetings in Scotland. A fellow passenger struck up a conversation and asked about a typical program sequence at the Billy Graham Crusade. As I was describing how the meetings were conducted, I found myself at a loss for words when I tried to describe the responses that usually accompanied Mr. Graham's invitation to become a Christian. All I could say was, what happens then never becomes commonplace, watching people by the hundreds come forward. Oh, if you could just see the wonder of it all! That night I began to ponder that thought and I wrote the lyrics and melody:*

There's the wonder of sunset at evening,
The wonder as sunrise I see;
But the wonder of wonders that thrills my soul,
Is the wonder that God loves me!

Oh, the wonder of it all,
The wonder of it all,
Just to think that God loves me!
Just to think that God loves me!"

When you discover the wonder of God's love for you and His wonderful assignment for you, you discover the wonder of life and that is the Wonderful Counselor, almighty God, the everlasting Father, and the Prince of peace. You are God's witness and are armed with His message to take to the world. This is what real life is all about.

Paul writes in **Philippians 3:8 CEV:** *"Nothing is as wonderful as knowing Christ Jesus my Lord."* and in **2 Corinthians 4:1, *The Living Bible*,** *"It is God himself, in his mercy, who has given us this wonderful work [of telling his Good News to others], and so we never give up."*

Have you discovered the wonder of life? I wonder?

Think about it. *Selah!*

Day 34: Hiding God's Word In Your Heart

"I have hidden your word in my heart, that I might not sin against you. . . . Open my eyes to see, the wonderful truths in your instructions. I am only a foreigner in the land. Don't hide your commands from me!" **Psalm 119:11 & 18-19 NLT**

Have you memorized Scripture? Can you quote verses or passages of Scripture by memory? When situations arise in your life, do you think of a verse or passage that seems to address that situation?

Memorizing Scripture is a must for the believer. If you have not memorized Scripture, then you will have questions, problems and doubts about God and life. If you haven't memorized before, then start now. God's Word is important. Here is what one of the greatest American thinkers, Jonathan Edwards, has written in a sermon that was given to the Mohawk Indians on the Scripture **2 Timothy 3:16,** *"All Scripture is given of God . . . : "* *'Tis worth the while to take a great deal of pains to learn to read and understand the Scriptures. I would have all of you think this. When there is such a book that you may have, how can you be contented without being able to read it?*

"How does it make you feel when you think there is a Book that is God's own Word? Parents should take care that their children learn . . . this will be the way to be kept from the Devil . . . But if you let the Word of God alone, and never use it, you can't expect the benefits of it. You must not only hear and read it but you must have it sunk

down into your heart . . . . You must endeavor to understand . . . Consider how much it is worth the while to go often to your Bible to hear the great God Himself speak to you. There you may hear God speak. How much better we think this is than the word of men. Better than the word of the wisest man of the world."

Think about it. *Selah!*

Day 35: Pray For Your Enemy

"Moreover, as for me, far be it from me that I should sin against the Lord in ceasing to pray for you: but I will teach you the good and the right way." **1 Samuel 12:23 NKJV**

"And who is my neighbor?" **Luke 10:29 ESV.** That was the follow-up question asked by the lawyer to Jesus in the Temple after having asked what was required to gain eternal life. The response of Jesus was: *"What is written in the law? How do you read it?"* **Luke 10:26 ESV.** The lawyer was looking for a loophole. Jesus was about to make a point.

Your neighbor is anyone that you meet, the people that you come in contact with each day. Your neighbor is your friend, your acquaintance, the good, the bad, the ugly, and your enemy, including the ones you love and the ones you hate. Your neighbor is both those who like you and those who hate you.

It's easy to pray for friends, family and good neighbors. It is another thing to pray for those who despitefully use you, **Matthew 5:11-12**. That person who irritates you and who you just have no affection for at all, that person is hard for you to pray for. But Jesus tells us that we should love and pray for our enemies. **Luke 6:27-28**

In **1 Samuel 12:23,** the prophet Samuel prays for the nation of Israel after they had insulted God by asking for a king. Samuel said: *"Moreover, as for me, far be it from*

me that I should sin against the Lord in ceasing to pray for you; but I will teach you the good and the right way."
1 Samuel 12:23 NKJV

The people sinned and needed prayer and guidance. Those people, who despitefully use you and even your enemy, need to be shown the better way, the right way, and the way of truth and life. Those people need Jesus Christ and you are His ambassador. An ambassador brings the response of his king, not his own private opinion.

The lawyer in the Temple needed to know that even the Samaritans, his opponents, and the opposition that he hated were his neighbors. The lawyer was not doing what was required to have eternal life. The Samaritans needed eternal life, and the lawyer and the leaders of the Temple needed eternal life.

What this says to us is that we are commanded to pray for our enemies. We are to pray for the worst of society as well as the best of society. It is a sin if we do not pray for them.

Think about it. *Selah!*

Day 36: Having Trouble Sleeping?

"Jesus was sleeping at the back of the boat with his head on a cushion. The disciples woke him up, shouting, 'Teacher, don't you care that we're going to drown?' "
Mark 4:38 NLT

I remember so many times having worked hard and long on a musical program and losing sleep wondering what was going to happen? It seems as though everything and everyone was working against me. Nothing seemed to be going right; but when the final note was played, the final act had come to an end, and the sweat begins to subside, my thoughts were: "I don't know what happened, but it worked!" What happened is God stepped in and took over.

The truth here is this: *"having done your best, give God the rest."* If we have been faithful in doing the work that was required to prepare for worship, then it is time to release the results to The Faithful One. God does not disappoint, He fulfills. God is not worried about the conclusion. He is the conclusion, and He does not disappoint, He fulfills. God does frustrate and disappoint the schemes of the wicked to bring about their failure, **Job 5:12.**

When all is going wrong, be confident that it is God's turn now. Remember when the disciples were out in the boat on the Sea of Galilee? A storm arose and they felt as though the boat was about to sink, **Mark 4:37-38.** Well, it wasn't about to sink. Jesus was in that boat and the same storm that caused the disciples to become frantic with worry, rocked Jesus to sleep. They forgot that the Storm-Stopper, the Peacemaker, had everything in control.

Did you know that this same Jesus has everything under control in your life as well? If you have done your best in the work that God has called you to do, then trust Him, don't frantically complain to Him: "Master, don't you care about me, I'm about to die?" You will not die until Jesus allows it. Don't wonder, where is God? God is with you and He is in the same boat that you are in. So, do your best and then give God the rest!

When storms come, just rest on the pillow of God's faithfulness. You just need to trust Him. He's the Faithful One.

Think about it. *Selah!*

Day 37: Have You Come To A Barrier?

"And behold, the curtain of the temple was torn in two, from top to bottom. And the earth shook, and the rocks were split." **Matthew 27:51 ESV**

Have you ever experienced times in your life where it seems you have come against a barrier that will not allow you to make the advances, or progress, that you feel you need to make? Does it seem as though your goal, aim, or objective is being hindered?

Remember this: *"Behold I have set before you an open door, which no one is able to shut. I know that you have but little power, and yet you have kept my word and have not denied my name."* **Revelation 3:8 ESV**

You might allow something to hinder you but no one can hinder God. At times, though, God can hinder or slow you down so "go with His flow," not the world's flow. God has taken down the curtain that used to be a barrier between God and man, but it is down now. Go to God boldly and make your request known to Him, and then step back and wait on Him.

I like what John MacArthur says in his Study Bible comments on **Matthew 27:51**: "Jesus broke down the barrier so you could break through whatever holds you back and allow Him to break in to the broken places in your life."

Sometimes what we may perceive to be barriers in our ministry may be boundaries or parameters set by

God. It could be a voice behind us pointing out the correct path: "That isn't the way; this is the way, walk in this path." **Isaiah 30:21**

We have direct access to the Father, and the Holy Spirit is at our side to teach us, to prepare us, and to lead us in the path that we should go. He does set boundaries or parameters for us in our work for Him, but those parameters are set to focus our power upon the objective.

We aren't hindered by the world. We are sent into the world in the power of God's might and the authority of His word.

Think about it. *Selah!*

Day 38: The Red Line

"Don't be fooled by what they say. For that day will not come until there is a great rebellion against God and the man of lawlessness is revealed—the one who brings destruction. He will exalt himself and defy everything that people call god and every object of worship. He will even sit in the temple of God, claiming that he himself is God. Don't you remember that I told you about all this when I was with you? And you know what is holding him back, for he can be revealed only when his time comes. For this lawlessness is already at work secretly, and it will remain secret until the one who is holding it back steps out of the way." **2 Thessalonians 2:3-7 NLT**

Do you remember the challenge boys would often make? A boy would draw a line in the dirt and proclaim: "Don't step over that line!" To step over the line would bring about one of two things: wrath and battle or it would reveal a bluff.

We have witnessed leaders of countries proclaim a line-in-the-sand or a red line, and the challenge was taken, but it was not followed by wrath and it revealed a bluff, nothing but words. A bluff only fans the fire; wrath stops aggression. The one drawing the line must be able to back up his challenge with sure and sudden wrath.

We read in **Job 1:12 and 2:6** where God drew a line, set limits or held back the acts of Satan. Satan did not cross a line that was drawn by God because he knew God says what he means and means what he says and if his line was crossed, sudden and sure wrath would follow.

The believer needs to know that Satan can do only what the Holy Spirit permits him to do. He needs to know that the Holy Spirit will take whatever Satan does and use it for God's good and our security. The believer is safe in the hand of God and the believer must keep this fact at the forefront of his mind.

Satan will, one day, be unleashed for a time and during that time he will wreak his wrath upon God's messengers and their followers. But that time will not come until the One who is holding him back, the Holy Spirit, is taken out of his way.

God has drawn a line upon your life and has told Satan, "Don't step over this line!" Satan will not make a move because he knows that God means what He says and will back His word up with sure and sudden wrath. He has also given the believer all that is needed to stand in the midst of Satan's destructive acts.

Think about it. *Selah!*

Day 39: The Bible And The Gospel

"But my life is worth nothing to me unless I use it for finishing the work assigned me by the Lord Jesus—the work of telling others the Good News about the wonderful grace of God." **Acts 20:24 NLT**

Did you know that the Bible is written to the believer? It contains within it the expectations of God toward those who follow Him, the believers. He expects holiness and righteousness. It is not written to non-believers for they deny His existence and do not know Him and cannot come to Him unless they are drawn by Him. *"For no one can come to me unless the Father who sent me draws them to me, and at the last day I will raise them up."* **John 6:44 NLT**

God the Father sent His Son Jesus Christ into this world with Good News. The Good News was that Jesus would live a sinless life, die, and then rise again to pay mankind's sin debt. God expects holiness and righteousness, yet mankind is unholy and unrighteous. This sin gap between God and man would be bridged by Jesus, who would "take up the slack" between what God expected and mankind's inability to meet those expectations. This is Good News for all mankind!

When Jesus ascended to heaven, He told his followers, those who believed in Him, that He was leaving with us this Good News, this Gospel to take to the entire world. It would be an invitation for all to repent and receive and to turn around from where they were going to where God wants them to go. It was to give light in their darkness and meaningless life.   It offers forgiveness.

So, this is our work, the work of telling to others the Good News about God's wonderful kindness and love. Are you involved? If not, shouldn't you be?

Think about it. *Selah!*

Day 40: The Supreme Court

"Therefore, God elevated him to the place of highest honor and gave him the name above all other names, that at the name of Jesus every knee should bow, in heaven and on earth and under the earth, and every tongue declare that Jesus Christ is Lord, to the glory of God the Father." **Philippians 2:9-11 NLT**

We believers in Jesus Christ who live in the United States of America have been upset frequently by rulings made by our Supreme Court. We are upset because they continue to make rulings which become laws that directly contradict the writings of the Bible.

Our reason for being upset is well founded, but perhaps we need to take a closer look at what is happening. The Supreme Court of these United States of America is supreme only in the United States. It affects no other people. God, however, is supreme everywhere. There is no place that is exempt from being subject to His Word and to His decrees.

Believers need not worry about the ruling of a limited court because its jurisdiction is not far reaching. But know this: all are subject to God's jurisdiction and His all encompassing hand. All nations will bow before Him. The work of the believer is to take this ruling of God, the Chief Justice, to the lost and dying world. Have you been faithful in taking this Good News to the world? The Good News is a pardon for sin, a setting free of the penalty of sin. This is an important ruling, but the pardon has a stipulation, a caveat, which is that it must be accepted or rejected.

We must pray for our Supreme Court. They are not bad people they are blind people. They are faithfully expressing what they humanly understand, believe, and know. They need the light of Jesus in their lives, and without His light they cannot see. They need to know God, submit to his Word, and uphold his Word.

Pray for the Supreme Court and the leaders of our land. They really cannot see, and they only rule on that which they do see. One more thing, be diligent to obey Jesus and take His Good News to the lost and dying around you that they may know God, take His offer of forgiveness, and receive His eternal life. If you remain silent, you are holding back the Good News that you have been entrusted with. The believer has the light, and we need to be faithful in spreading and expressing what we understand, believe, and know.

Are you faithful and diligent in spreading the Good News?

Think about it. *Selah!*

Day 41: Of Such Is The Kingdom Of God

". . . Let the children come to me. Don't stop them! For the kingdom of God belongs to those who are like these children. I tell you the truth, anyone who doesn't receive the Kingdom of God like a child will never enter it." **Mark 10:14-15 NLT**

Children come into this world without fear and with total faith. They learn to fear, and they learn to distrust by repeated broken promises and the many disappointments that they experience in life. The older they become, the more their fears increase and the less their faith becomes.

We see the same scenario worked out with the new believer as well. When people first receive Jesus Christ as Lord and Savior, they have total and unquestioned faith in living the Christian life, but as they begin to experience the faithlessness of other believers and see the fear that they have allowed in their lives, their faith begins to weaken.

What the Christian believer needs to do is quit doing things that cause new believers to lose faith in trusting God. The strong believer needs to strengthen the weaker believer or new believer. The stronger believer should be actively doing things that confirm the weaker and younger believer's faith and trust in God. Don't do things to hinder them or forbid them from becoming strong.

"... *Let the children come to me. Don't stop them! For the kingdom of God belongs to those who are like these children. I tell you the truth, anyone who doesn't receive the Kingdom of God like a child will never enter it.*" **Mark 10:14-15 NLT**

Think about it. *Selah!*

Day 42: Put The Blame Where It Belongs

"So the law is holy, and the commandment is holy and righteous and good. Did that which is good, then, bring death to me? By no means! It was sin, producing death in me through what is good, in order that sin might be shown to be sin, and through the commandment might become sinful beyond measure" **Romans 7:12-13 ESV**

The Law defines God's righteousness. God is pure. He is holy and good and unless you have been covered with the righteousness of God, you cannot enter His heaven. Every person who is born into this world is born into sin and is unworthy of the presence of God because of sin.   We read this in God's Word: *"for all have sinned and fall short of the glory of God,"* **Romans 3:23 NKJV,** and *"There is none righteous, no, not one;"* **Romans 3:10 NKJV.**

The only way for an earthly created being to be righteous is to be made a new creation of God. This old creation is dead in sin and must be made alive in a new creation. *"And you He made alive, who were dead in trespasses and sins, in which you once walked according to the course of this world, according to the prince of the power of the air, the spirit who now works in the sons of disobedience, among whom also we all once conducted ourselves . . ."* **Ephesians 2:1-3 NKJV.**

God made us righteous by putting our sin on Jesus and placing Jesus' righteousness upon us, **2 Corinthians 5:21.** Since you cannot have a do-over in life on earth, God has given us a new-over. Old things are passed away and all things are become new.

Don't despise the Law and Commandments of God for they are holy, righteous, and good. Hate sin, which the Law and Commandments of God reveal.

Repent of those sins and receive in exchange the righteousness of Christ Jesus our Lord.

Think about it. *Selah!*

Day 43: Out Of Our Sight

"I thank God whom I serve, as did my ancestors, with a clear conscience, as I remember you constantly in my prayers night and day. As I remember your tears, I long to see you, that I may be filled with joy." **2 Timothy 1:3-4 ESV**

Jonathan Edwards had sent his nine-year-old son, Jonathan Jr., with Gideon Hawley to the Delaware territory to help in the work with the Delaware Indians, which was some two hundred miles away from Stockbridge, Massachusetts. He sent him there to learn the Mohawk language. The following letter was written:

"Though you are a great way off from us, yet you are not out of our minds: I am full of concern for you, often think of you, and often pray for you. Though you are at so great a distance from us, and from all your relations, yet this is a comfort to us, that the same God that is here is also at Onohoquaha and that though you are out of our sight, and out of our reach, you are always in God's hands, who is infinitely gracious; and we can go to Him, and commit you to His care and mercy. Take heed that you don't forget or neglect Him. Always set God before your eyes, and live in His fear, and seek Him every day with all diligence: for He, and He only can make you happy or miserable, as he pleases; and your Life and Health, and the eternal salvation of your soul and your all in this life and that which is to come depends on His will and pleasure."

I have children, family, and friends that I love who are thousands of miles away but I know that they cannot be out of the touch of my great God. When you pray to God for one of your loved ones, be confident that He is presently with them as He is presently with you. Though you are incapable of putting your arms around them, God has His around them and comforts them where they are. As sure as your thoughts and prayers are with those loved ones, so is God with them.

Think about it. *Selah!*

Day 44: Remembrance, What's On Your Mind?

"For this reason we also, since the day we heard it, do not cease to pray for you, and to ask that you may be filled with the knowledge of His will in all wisdom and spiritual understanding;" **Colossians 1:9 NKJV**

Memory can bring back good events or bad events that took place in our past. Memory is a replay button that we can use to bring about a smile or a frown, a happy moment or a hurtful moment of the past. How often have you said to a friend, "Do you remember when [fill in the blank]?"

We are encouraged by some memories and repulsed by others. Our memories bring back lessons learned and truths confirmed. I like what King David said about God's memory of him in **Psalm 139:17 NKJV** *"How precious also are Your thoughts to me, O God! How great is the sum of them!"* When God thinks of us, His thoughts are thoughts of love and laughter. When He thinks of us, He thinks of Jesus. He thinks of Jesus because we are covered with His righteousness. **2 Corinthians 5:21**

Paul frequently tells those to whom he was writing a letter or Epistle that his thoughts toward them are thoughts that bring about prayers of thanksgiving.

So, what are you remembering right now? Are your thoughts those that bring encouragement or discouragement? Are your thoughts those that are precious or resentful? May I suggest that if those thoughts bring about sadness, discouragement and unpleasantness, then you should forget them. They are only causing you harm **(Psalm 37:8).** Those thoughts are not from God but Satan. Ask God to remove them from your mind and replace them with thoughts of laughter, joy, comfort, and encouragement. May your thoughts be of those special people that God has placed into your life. If your thoughts are of God continually, you will be having thoughts of love, joy, gentleness, patience, faithfulness, goodness, longsuffering, and self-control. These are the fruits of the Spirit **(Galatians 5:22-23).** All other thoughts are of the works of the flesh **(Galatians 5:19-21).**

James 4:7-8 tells us to *"draw near to God and He will draw near to"* us and to *"resist the Devil and he will flee"* **NKJV**. So, resist the inclination that you may have to remember hurtful events and rest in the good thoughts that come from God. Having done that, be thankful to God, remembering that He has been so good.

Think about it. *Selah!*

Day 45: How Much Sin Will God Forgive?

"You were dead because of your sins and because your sinful nature was not yet cut away. Then God made you alive with Christ, for he forgave all our sins. He canceled the record of the charges against us and took it away by nailing it to the cross. In this way, he disarmed the spiritual rulers and authorities. He shamed them publicly by his victory over them on the cross." **Colossians 2:13-15 NLT**

How much sin will God forgive? Are you a great sinner? John Newton's life spanned the years of 1725 – 1807. For the first part of his life, he was a sailor in the Royal Navy of England and then the captain of a slave ship. He was a vicious, brutal, immoral man who took great pride in his debauchery. After he received Jesus Christ as his Savior, it was a great turnaround. At the age of 82, he had lost all his sight but had gained great spiritual sight. He made note: *"My memory is nearly gone, but I remember two things: That I am a great sinner, and that Christ is a great Savior."*

Another great sinner the Apostle Paul, who called himself *"the chief of sinners,"* wrote in his letter to the Colossian church that Christ Jesus *"canceled the record of the charges against us"* **Colossians 2:14 NLT.**

How much sin does God forgive? He forgives all of it. **Romans 5:20** tells us that where the stronghold of sin was rampant, grace did much more run rampant. **Psalm 103:12** tells us that God removed our sins from us as far as the east is from the west. When God does something, he does it exceedingly, abundantly and far above our meager ability to do or think. · **Ephesians 3:20**

Horatio Spafford's well-known hymn "It is Well With My Soul" contains the lines:

> *My sin—oh, the bliss of this glorious thought:*
> *My sin—not in part, but the whole*
> *Is nailed to the cross and I bear it no more,*
> *Praise the Lord, praise the Lord, O my soul!*

John Newton was right. We do have a great Savior! Here is the truth: How much sin does God forgive? As much as his love, grace, and mercy is able to cleanse, and that is far more than the ability of man to sin. His grace is sufficient!

Think about it. *Selah!*

Day 46: A Mind That Is Stayed On God

"You keep him in perfect peace whose mind is stayed on you, because he trusts in you. Trust in the Lord forever, for the Lord God is an everlasting rock."
Isaiah 26:3-4 ESV

What is the promise of Jesus to His disciples and followers concerning what we should expect in this present world in which we live? He said:

> *In the world you will have trouble, **John 16:33**
> *Men will hate you, **John 15:18**
> *Men will scatter you, **John 16:32**
> *You are not of this world, **John 15:19**.

But what did He promise us? He assured us of:

> *A new place to live, **John 14:2-3**
> *Peace in the midst of trouble while we are waiting on Him, **John 14:27**
> **& John 16:33**.

So, if we are to expect trouble, how is it that we are to experience this peace that Jesus is talking about? The answer is trust. We trust in what Jesus has said and take confidence in those promises. If we expect trouble, then we are not shocked by it when it appears. We should also expect an awesome supply of peace to counteract that trouble.

Isaiah talks of that peace: *"You keep him in perfect peace whose mind is stayed on you, because he trusts in*

you. Trust in the Lord forever, for the Lord God is an everlasting rock." **Isaiah 26:3-4 ESV**

The Apostle James speaks to it: *"Draw near to God, and he will draw near to you. Cleanse your hands, you sinners, and purify your hearts you double-minded,"* **James 4:8 ESV.**

There is no sorrow in the presence of Jesus. **Psalm 16:11 ESV** says: *"You make known to me the path of life; in your presence there is fullness of joy; at your right hand are pleasures forevermore."* In **Psalm 30:5 ESV** we find that *". . . weeping may tarry for the night, but joy comes with the morning."*

What I am saying is this: The believer in Jesus Christ is going to experience trouble while on this earth; expect it. But while in the grip of great sorrow, expect awesome peace and joy as you draw near to Jesus. If you enter the courts of Jesus, you can only have joy and praise. The peace that passes all understanding that Jesus was talking about is always present in His presence. Look to Jesus, the author and finisher of your faith, keep your eyes upon Him, and you will find that your feet are securely placed on the Rock of Jesus. Jesus' part is the promise of peace. Our part is the drawing near, the entering in, and the abiding in Him. If you have done that, you will have perfect peace, and you can handle any trouble that Satan may bring your way.

Think about it. *Selah!*

Day 47: Silent Before God

"And after the earthquake a fire, but the Lord was not in the fire. And after the fire the sound of a low whisper."
1 Kings 19:12 ESV

Randy Alcorn shares a story about meeting a student of his who was taking a seminary course he was teaching on the theology of heaven.   The student had been a pastor for twenty years prior to his entering the seminary. The pastor told Randy that God had given him a perfect life for twenty years and then his son died. For several months following his son's death, he would go before the Lord and shout questions such as: *"Why? What have I done to deserve this?   What were you thinking God? How am I supposed to preach to others of the great love of God?   Then, he said, as I became silent before the Lord, I began to hear God speak . . . without any announcement, when I became silent, God spoke to my soul and answered all my questions."*

Job experienced that still small voice, as did Elijah and many more that we read of in Scripture. One of the most fruitful things that a person can do is to sit silently before God and listen. He will speak softly and quietly to us. As He places His great arms around us and pulls us close to Him, it is then that we hear the strong and comforting voice of God as He speaks peace to our soul. He answers our questions personally as only He can. When He speaks the storm must go away.

Have you come to a place of silence before God? Have you just stood silently before God or knelt before

Him, lying prostrate to allow Him to come to you and speak? It is at times like this that we hear the still small voice of God in our ear. *"And the things of earth will grow strangely dim in the light of his glory and grace."* (Helen H. Lemmel, "Turn Your Eyes Upon Jesus")

Think about it. *Selah!*

Day 48: An Inadequate Faith

"But if God so clothes the grass of the field, which today is alive and tomorrow is thrown into the oven, will he not much more clothe you, O you of little faith?" **Matthew 6:30 ESV**

In his book **The Goodness of God**, Randy Alcorn says: *"Evil and suffering have a way of exposing our inadequate theology. When affliction comes, a weak or nominal Christian often discovers that his faith doesn't account for it or prepare him for it. His faith has been in his church, denomination, or family tradition, or in his own religious ideas—but not in Christ. As he faces evil and suffering, he may, in fact, lose his faith.*
But that's actually a good thing; any faith that leaves us unprepared for suffering is a false faith that deserves to be abandoned. Genuine faith will be tested by suffering; false faith will be lost—the sooner the better." That is an inadequate faith. It is unworthy of God. It is one that will not prevail in life.

Jesus on at least six different occasions chastened His disciples for their little or inadequate faith: **Matthew 6:30, Matthew 8:26, Matthew 14:31,** and **Matthew 16:8.** The situations were daily problems dealing with provisions that were needed in their lives, problems with the storms in their lives, times when they had to learn to trust in God with their lives, and overcome the doubts in their lives. In each of these events Jesus used the phrase: *"O you of little faith."*

Genuine faith prevails and overcomes everything that this world may throw at us, while an inadequate faith brings doubt, distrust, and stress. Why would we doubt God? If God promises us, then He will fulfill his promise. This is unnecessary fretting. In **Psalm 37**, the Psalmist warns us not to fret because it only causes harm.

What is it that brings stress in your life today? What is it that you are allowing to come between you and the all-sufficient Jesus? You can count on this, that stress is not of God because He left us His peace that exceeds all understanding. God's peace cancels the stressful things that we experience and it surpasses our ability to understand. Therefore, accept His peace, be thankful for His peace, and rest in the One who is able to do way beyond any expectation that you may have. That rest I have found in the person of Jesus.

Think about it. *Selah!*

Day 49: At Ease

"Woe to you who are at ease in Zion . . . " **Amos 6:1 NKJV**

The command "At Ease" means that the soldier is no longer at attention. It means he it at rest. In **Amos 6:1** the prophet Amos warns against being at rest. The **New Living Translation** puts it this way: *"What sorrow awaits you who lounge in luxury in Jerusalem, and you who feel secure in Samaria! You are famous and popular in Israel, and the people go to you for help."* Eugene Peterson paraphrases it: *"Woe to you who think you live on easy street in Zion."*

Here is the truth: We should not aspire to be easy street Christians—Christians who feel God's desire for us on earth is to live in luxury, to be financially secure in earthly terms, to press toward the goal of being famous, or aware of our own resourcefulness apart from God. Our desire as Christians should be to become obedient witnesses and ambassadors for our King, the Lord Jesus Christ, and that we would be found faithful doing what he has called us to do.

Don't rest in life and be at ease with luxury and easy living. Desire to have all that God has available for you in order to do all that He has personally called you to do in spreading His Good News, and then do it. This is the real meaning to life in Christ on this earth. Paul says in **Acts 20:24 NLT,** *"But my life is worth nothing to me unless I use it for finishing the work assigned me by the*

Lord Jesus—the work of telling others the Good News about the wonderful grace of God."

Are you at ease or at attention to the leading of the Holy Spirit in your life?

Think about it. *Selah!*

Day 50: Looking For The Extravagant And Ignoring The Essential

"Looking unto Jesus the author and finisher of our faith; who for the joy that was set before him endured the cross, despising the shame, and is set down at the right hand of the throne of God." **Hebrews 12:2 KJV**

I know you have heard this phrase: *"Sacrificing the permanent on the altar of the expedient."* It means that what seems to be the most important thing at the moment and under the present conditions often is not the thing that lasts and really matters in life. A good decision requires one to consider how that decision will affect the future. Scripture tells us that what seems right at the moment may not be the right thing at all, and it may actually lead to ones destruction. **Proverbs 16:25**

The essential thing is to seek good advice and to seek sure direction in life. The Holy Spirit is the believer's Guide in life, Comforter through life and Guarantee of eternal life. The Holy Spirit is the sure voice for a happy future. **Isaiah 30:21**

When Jesus left for heaven, He promised that He would not leave us comfortless and alone. He assured His followers that He would send the Holy Spirit as the believer's Comforter. He is the essential thing in life.

Don't look for the glossy, extravagant, and temporal things in life, but seek what is essential for life and eternity. The glossy and extravagant things blind the seeker in his quest for a life that matters and lasts. Jesus is the extravagant expression of God's love. *"Behold, what manner of love the Father hath bestowed upon us, that we should be called the sons of God . . ."* **1 John 3:1 KJV**.

Patti Miller Durham in her book, **Living Right Side Up in an Upside Down World,** makes this statement relating to discovering the essential things in life:

"In your need discover God as friend.
In your weakness discover God's strength and power.
In your loneliness discover God is your companion.
In our pain discover God is your comfort.
In your Confusion discover God as your stability and truth.
In your loss, discover God's ultimate love.
In your feelings of unworthiness, feel God's complete acceptance.
In your fear and devastation, discover God's comfort and security.
In your Feelings of shame, discover God's forgiveness."

Here is the truth: He who created all things is the extravagant one making an   extravagant sacrifice that we might secure an extravagant eternity. This is the essential thing in life, so seek it. You will find Him to be the answer to all the questions that life may bring.

Think about it. *Selah!*

Day 51: The Mysteries of God

"But it was to us that God revealed these things by his Spirit. For his Spirit searches out everything and shows us God's deep secrets . . . . But people who aren't spiritual can't receive these truths from God's Spirit. It all sounds foolish to them and they can't understand it, for only those who are spiritual can understand what the Spirit means. Those who are spiritual can evaluate all things, but they themselves cannot be evaluated by others." **1 Corinthians 2:10 & 14-15 NLT**

The mysteries of God are those things that are natural to Him, understood by Him, yet totally foreign to humanity, His creation. They are the things and the thoughts by His creation that go well beyond the creation's feeble field of knowledge and its ability to comprehend. Remember, we are the creation of God. We have creature minds, and we get frustrated trying to understand the thoughts of the uncreated Creator. They are mysteries to us.

So, God made a provision for us. He inspired and moved men of old, through the Holy Spirit, to express His mysterious and His inexpressible thoughts (**2 Peter 1:20-21**), thoughts that are beyond nature and thoughts that are part of nature itself.

When Jesus left for heaven, he sent the Holy Spirit to be our teacher (**John 16:5 –13).** The Holy Spirit uses human words that are "like" or the closest to the divine meaning.   The   believer   comes   to   a   spiritual understanding of these mysteries because they can only be spiritually understood and accepted by faith.

Mysteries must be revealed to a person in order for them to be understood, and until that time they remain a mystery. Never try to do the work of the Holy Spirit by attempting to explain the unexplainable to someone who is not a believer. Only the Holy Spirit can do that after a person becomes a believer. We have no words that are sufficient to define a mystery, so we accept it by faith. Faith is the substance of things hoped for and the evidence of things that are still yet to come, as the Bible tells us in **Hebrews 11:1.**

There are many things that we may question in life or that we do not understand about life, but we have a Counselor, a Teacher, a Comforter, and a Sustainer whom Jesus placed here for those questions that we have.

Take those mysterious things to God and ask Him about them, listen to Him and you will be able to rest in His counsel.

Think about it. *Selah!*

Day 52: Not A Matter Of Good Or Bad

"for all have sinned and fall short of the glory of God."
Romans 3:23 ESV

Jesus is the Great Physician. He is called the Great Physician because He deals with a great sickness that no other physician can deal with. He is the "The" Physician, because He is the one and only who holds the credentials, expertise, and complete cure to heal "The" disease, a disease that is greater than any pandemic that has ever ravished this earth. The disease is sin and all have sinned. Everyone has sinned, from Adam through the end of time. It was the first man Adam who brought about and contracted this disease, and then it spread to all, for all have sinned.

It is said that the Bubonic Plague, caused by the bacterium Yersinia pestis, claimed the lives of over 200 million people during the early 1330's. The fleas on rats and mice spread the Bubonic Plague to humanity; and sin is carried by heredity to all humanity. Some escaped the Bubonic Plague and some were immune to it, but no one escapes the disease of sin. No one is immune to it.

Jesus brought the cure and has it available to anyone who wants it. The cure is the blood of Jesus, and He shed it for all of humanity who would take it. The major point is you must realize and admit that you are affected and you are dying. You must know that there is no other cure and repent of any dependence you may have on anything or anyone else. Jesus is the only cure. You must do as the Great Physician says, and that is to love people as much as Jesus does and then tell other people of His great cure. You should want to live your life in a way that is pleasing to and reflective of "The Great Physician." This cure is sure and lasts for all eternity. It is a guaranteed cure and carries the Seal of the Holy Spirit of God.

There is no one who is beyond the point that this cure will not immediately and completely cure. It happens the moment that one takes it. So, what about you, have you taken the cure? Why not? Did you know that you are the very reason that Jesus, The Great Physician, came? You are His focus and His reason for dying.

I like what Ravi Zacharias has said: *"God did not send his only son into the world to make **bad** people **good** but to make **dead** people **alive**."*

The Apostle Paul tells us:

"for all have sinned and fall short of the glory of God," **Romans 3:23 ESV.**

> *"And you were dead in the trespasses and sins in which you once walked, following the course of this world,"* **Ephesians 2:1 ESV**

> *"But God, being rich in mercy, because of the great love with which he loved us, even when we were dead in our trespasses, made us alive*

together with Christ—by grace you have been saved." **Ephesians 2:4-5 ESV**

Here is the dosage: Take it all and take it now for now is the day of salvation, for now is your salvation sure. Obey His directions and listen to His voice as you visit the Great Physician. He makes house calls. Draw near to Him, trust his Word, read His Word, study his Word and abide in it. Pray at all times, resist the Devil, and he will flee, **James 4:7-8.**

That's it. God's glory will abide in you, and you will spend eternity in God's eternal day, free from all sin and unrighteousness. It's not about the good and bad; it's about your life, your eternal life, and the Great Physician has the cure.

Think about it. *Selah!*

Day 53: Let Them See Your Heart

"In the same way, let your good deeds shine out for all to see, so that everyone will praise your heavenly Father." **Matthew 5:16 NLT**

Did you know that the Bible is not written to the non-believer in Christ Jesus? The Bible is written to believers, and the Holy Spirit is the teacher of those things written within its pages. Since the unbelievers do not have the Holy Spirit within them, they cannot understand, and the believer should not expect them to understand.

The believer is the one called to take the Good News to the unbeliever. This is our assignment. *"But my life is worth nothing to me unless I use it for finishing the work assigned me by the Lord Jesus—the work of telling others the Good News about the wonderful grace of God,"* **Acts 20:24 NLT.** The Holy Spirit is the one who draws the non-believers to Jesus and convicts them of their sin. Joshua commanded the people to live an example life in the assignment God had given them: *" . . . Love the Lord your God, walk in all his ways, obey his commands, hold firmly to him, and serve him with all your heart and all your soul."* **Joshua 22:5b NLT**

Therefore, don't get ahead of the Holy Spirit and don't get frustrated when you do not see your expected result in doing your assignment of telling. Remember, the result is God's part and He does things in His own timing. Time means nothing to God but "timing" means everything. And there are some who will never respond to the Good News.

We are made in the image of God. The only image that people will see of God is the life we live before others. Jesus tells us that it is by His love that others will know we are His followers. So, let them see your heart of love. How you live matters and what you do matters, so be faithful in doing what really matters and what you have been assigned to do.

"In the same way, let your good deeds shine out for all to see, so that everyone will praise your heavenly Father." **Matthew 5:16 NLT**

Think about it. *Selah!*

Day 54: Remaining Happy And Being Content

"That's why I take pleasure in my weaknesses, and in the insults, hardships, persecutions, and troubles that I suffer for Christ. For when I am weak, then I am strong."
2 Corinthians 12:10 NLT

One of the most difficult things any individual will battle in life is the task to remain happy throughout life and to be content and patient in the times of struggle.

We would like to assume that people are basically and fundamentally good and have a desire to be good to all those around them. But this assumption is not true. The truth is that humanity is not basically and fundamentally good, but rather, it is fundamentally bad. We read in **Romans 3:23** "For all have sinned and come short of the glory of God;" **KJV**.

There is but one that is good and that one is God. Jesus told this to the man who called him *"Good Teacher"* as he asked Him about eternal life. *"And Jesus said to him, 'Why do you call me good? No one is good except God alone.' "* **Mark 10:18 ESV**

Not only are people fundamentally bad, this world is bad, and it is under the command of Satan, the prince and power of the air. Therefore, we should expect hardship, persecution, and calamities while in this world. Jesus also told us that we should expect trouble. In **John 16:33,** He also added that we should be of good cheer as we endure that trouble. Peace in the midst of a storm and happiness come from peace.

John Piper has said: *"The power of Christ is revealed in the ability of His followers to be insulted and remain happy."* How we endure difficult times is how we can relate to those who do not know Christ and how we can encourage those Christians who may struggle from time to time at a point of weakness. We who are strong ought to help those who are weak.

If you have not experienced trouble and weakness, you will at sometime. So, be of good cheer and be content or patient for in weakness you receive power. Be happy in Christ Jesus and let Him use you.

Things that happen to you may surprise you, but they do not surprise God nor do they alter in any way His plan for you. You are totally equipped for your assignment, so don't give in, don't give up, and never turn away from that which God has for you.

Think about it. *Selah!*

Day 55: Future Blessing Is Dependent Upon Our Present Obedience

"God blesses those who are poor and realize their need for him . . . God blesses those who mourn . . . God blesses those who are humble . . . God blesses those who hunger and thirst for justice . . . God blesses those who are merciful . . . God blesses those whose hearts are pure . . . God blesses those who work for peace . . . God blesses those who are persecuted . . . God blesses you when people mo k you and persecute you and lie about you . . . because you are my followers. Be happy about it! Be very glad! For a great reward awaits you in heaven. And remember, the ancient prophets were persecuted in the same way." **Matthew 5:3 – 11 NLT**

No one enjoys being criticized or taken advantage of or being made light of. The sad thing is that this is part of life. Everyone will experience all of these things often in their life. How we deal with those things will determine how we live and how happy we are. Happiness is a choice, and joy is a result of happiness. Sadness is a choice, and depression is the result of it.

For the believer and follower of Jesus Christ, we have One who goes along with us in life and helps us, comforts us, guides us, and instructs us. He is the Holy Spirit that Jesus left us. In **John 14: 15-17**, Jesus gives a caveat for taking advantage of this gift, and that is *"If you love me, obey my commandments. And I will ask the Father, and he will give you another Advocate . . . ."* **NLT**.

There is a blessing in obeying and following Jesus and that is He will counteract any difficulty with a blessing.

So, what am I saying? I am saying that the believer must expect opposition in life. The believer is opposed because Jesus was opposed, but in the opposition there is an abundant supply of blessing, peace, comfort, guidance, and love that comes down from the Father to His children.

So, be happy and receive the joy, the blessing and the peace of God in the midst of your life. Jesus knows all about you and all the things that have happened to you, are happening to you now, and will happen to you. He has made all the necessary arrangements for you to be victorious in your life through it all.

Andre Crouch addresses this thought in his song: *"Through it all, through it all, I've learned to trust in Jesus, I've learned to trust in God."*

Think about it. *Selah!*

Day 56: The Golden Rule

"Do to others whatever you would like them to do to you. This is the essence of all that is taught in the law and the prophets." **Matthew 7:12 NLT**

How do you respond to the people you meet in your everyday life? Do you get upset when things don't go your way? Author Nik Ripken in his book, <u>The Insanity of God,</u> writes about believers serving Jesus under severe persecution and returning the love of God for the brutality and torture that they received even as their earthly lives were taken from them. How were they able to do this?

Ripken tells of the account of Dmitri, a Russian Christian in a concentration prison where he was brutally punished and ridiculed for his faith by the guards as well as his fellow prisoners who would laugh, curse, jeer, and throw food and sometimes human waste to try to shut him up and extinguish the only true light shining in that dark place. Every morning for seventeen years he would stand at his bed, face the east toward his home, raise his hands and sing his "HeartSong," as he called it, to the Lord in the grip of those guards and fellow prisoners. But at the end as Dmitri was dragged from his cell, "down the corridor in the center of the prison, the strangest thing happened. Before they reached the door leading to the courtyard— before stepping out into the place of execution—fifteen hundred hardened criminals stood at attention by their beds. They faced the east and they began to sing." One of the guards "demanded to know, 'Who are you?'

Dmitri straightened his back and stood as tall and as proud as he could. He responded: 'I am a son of the Living God, and Jesus is His name!' " (<u>The Insanity of God,</u> page 158). He was not executed but was taken back to his cell. He was later released, and he returned to his family.

Dmitri did not rebel. He obeyed his God and offered them the Good News. He gave those individuals that which made all the difference in his life. He offered them love, and he offered to them that which means the most in life, the Good News.

How have you been treated? How have you responded to those God has brought into your life? The Golden rule is to do unto others what you would like for them to do to you. If you were where they are, wouldn't you want to know about the Good News?

Think about it. *Selah!*

Day 57: One Thing

"I will meditate on your precepts and fix my eyes on your ways. I will delight in your statutes; I will not forget your word." **Psalm 119:15-16 ESV**

In **Isaiah 26:3 ESV** we read: *"You keep him in perfect peace, whose mind is stayed on you, because he trusts in you."* I think we have lost the art of focusing on *one thing*, in doing *one thing*, and in doing it well. Multi-tasking is the word of our day and we value the individual most who is able to take on the most. Because of this our lives have become crowded and the simple values that once were coveted are no longer in vogue. We are okay with letting them go that more might be done. We find our lives divided and out of focus. In our quest to accomplish much, we have lost the art of focusing on one thing. God is no longer important because He requires our worship, and He alone is worthy of any glory in life.

We find our families to be just another task in life and, therefore, they fall apart. Tommy Walker penned these lyrics of his worship song, "I Fix My Eyes On You":

> *I fix my eyes on You, the Author of my faith,*
> > *Casting aside every sin and every weight.*
> *I fix my eyes on you, I lay my burdens down*
> > *Letting the cares of this world now fade away.*

Let me ask this of you: Fix your eyes on Christ today. Look into His holy face, ask Him to take control of your day, and then let Him do it. Forget all else and fix your eyes upon His Word. Fix your eyes on doing that assignment that He has given you to do. Did you know He doesn't ask you to do multiple things but to do *one thing*. Whatever that *one thing* is, do it and let Him do the rest.

The world and even the church itself will ask you to do other things, but may I suggest that you focus on *one thing*. Paul says in **Philippians 3:13-14 ESV,** *"Brothers, I do not consider that I have made it my own. But one thing I do: forgetting what lies behind and straining forward to what lies ahead, I press on toward the goal for the prize of the upward call of God in Christ Jesus."*

Think about it. *Selah!*

Day 58: Is Everyone Really Against You?

"When the servant of the man of God rose early in the morning and went out, behold, an army with horses and chariots was all around the city. And the servant said, 'Alas, my master! What shall we do?' He said, 'Do not be afraid, for those who are with us are more than those who are with them.' Then Elisha prayed and said, 'O Lord, please open his eyes that he may see.' So the Lord opened the eyes of the young man, and he saw, and behold, the mountain was full of horses and chariots of fire all around Elisha." **2 Kings 6:15-17 ESV**

What do you see in your life? Do you see mountains of difficulties, problems, oppressions and struggles that resist you in your pursuits in life and doing the assignment that God has given you to do, or do you see opportunities that have been strategically placed in your life to challenge you, strengthen you, train you, and to develop resilience and character in your life and equip you for the assignment that God has given you? How one views life and how one approaches life will determine how happy and successful he is.

The truth of life is that what you see at the moment may not be a clear representation of what is actually happening. It may not be apparent to you at the moment, but there are more people for you and on your side than you realize.

We read in the Bible that if God is for us, this is all that really matters. *"What then shall we say to these*

things? If God is for us, who can be against us?" **Romans 8:31 ESV**

Did you know that God places people in our lives to help us and to encourage us as we serve him? Did you know that it is Satan who puts people in our lives to discourage us and prevent us from doing the assignment God has given us to do? This is the great battle we face in life, but you can be certain that there are more for us than there are against us.

The believer's problem is that it is the vocal and "in your face" people among us who seem to grab our attention and want center stage. It is those temporary and soon to be gone people who cause us to close our eyes to the real, the permanent, and the sure things in our lives. The Apostle Paul addresses this temptation as he writes in **Romans 8:31**, *"What then shall we say to these things?"* What we should do is to refer them to our God, our sure defense and their Judge. Remember, God is for us and there is nothing that can separate us from God or cause Him to change His mind. If God knows all things, He does not need to change His decided course of action. Believe God. Reject all else.

There are many people who oppose the believer, but all that we need to know is that our God has given us more than we need to be victorious in life. *"He said, 'Do not be afraid, for those who are with us are more than those who are with them.' "*
2 Kings 6:16 ESV

"No, in all these things we are more than conquerors through him who loves us. For I am sure that neither death nor life, nor angels nor rulers, nor things present nor things to come, nor powers, nor height nor depth, nor anything else in all creation, will be able to separate us from the love of God in Christ Jesus our Lord." **Romans 8:37-39 ESV**

Think about it. *Selah!*

Day 59: His Extravagant Love

"See what kind of love the Father has given to us, that we should be called children of God; and so we are." **1 John 3:1 ESV**

Extravagant is defined as lacking restraint in spending money or using resources. It is costing too much and exceeding what is reasonable or appropriate; it is absurd.

Extravagant, that is the type of love that God has for us. While we were still ungodly sinners, sinning extravagantly, selfish, uncaring, unaware, and without help, Christ died for us. **Romans 5:6; Ephesians 2:5**

God's love is extravagant and was lavishly poured out upon us, but it is not thoughtlessly given. It was poured out for all to take, but with the knowledge that most people would reject that extravagant love. Now that is love, extravagant love. It is love that is flooded upon mankind without restraint. It is too high a price and definitely exceeds what would be considered reasonable and appropriate. It really is absurd, but it is God's absurdity. It is an absurd display of His great heart for mankind. He spared no expense. Just as the actions of the prodigal son stand in stark contrast to the love of his father for him, so the Heavenly Father extravagantly loves us.

Yes, God loves you! Why? It is because He wants to. He loves you with a love beyond human description, with His extravagant love. Now all you need to do to be a recipient of that love is to accept it. He takes your sin and in exchange He gives you His righteousness. He takes your bad reputation and gives you His reputation. He takes your inability to be worthy and gives you His faithfulness and makes you worthy of the presence of God. That is His plan, and He wants you to have it.

Do you have it? You can, if you will humble yourself before Him and admit that you are a sinner beyond help, admit that you are ungodly, and desire to be godly. If you will admit that Jesus is God's Son, that He died to pay the price for your sins, that He rose from the grave to secure your salvation and is coming back to take you to be with Him for eternity, then His extravagant love will be realized in your life.

"See what kind of love the Father has given to us, that we should be called children of God; and so we are."
1 John 3:1 ESV

Think about it. *Selah!*

Day 60: God Always Seems Bigger To Those Who Need Him Most

"But while in deep distress, Manasseh sought the Lord his God and sincerely humbled himself before the God of his ancestors. And when he prayed, the Lord listened to him and was moved by his request. So the Lord brought Manasseh back to Jerusalem and to his kingdom. Then Manasseh finally realized that the Lord alone is God!" **2 Chronicles 33:12-13**

Manasseh was the son of good king Hezekiah. He was only 12 years old when he became king and he reigned for 55 years. He is arguably the most wicked king of Judah (696 BC – 642 BC). He did evil and was involved in detestable heathen practices and led Judah in those practices.

Although he was raised by a godly father, he was influenced by the ungodly and developed a life of ungodliness and total evil. His luxurious life-style led to his turning away from God, and it was not until he found himself in deep distress and insufficiency that he found the sufficiency of God. When he turned to God, God listened and God turned his life around.

God always listens. We may deny God and live lives of godlessness, but it is when hardships come that they seem to press us up toward God. It is when we find ourselves without hope we look to the sure hope that is found in Christ Jesus.

When we have our backs turned away from God, we cannot see Him. Although we cannot see Him, it does not mean that He is not there or doesn't exist.

This prayer was found scratched on a cellar wall in Cologne, Germany, by a Jew hiding from Nazi persecution:

I believe in the sun,
Even when it is not shining.
I believe in love,
Even when I feel it not.
I believe in God,
Even when there is silence.

Do you feel God is far from you? Turn your eyes to Him and you will discover that He is right there with you, as big as ever.

Think about it. *Selah!*

Day 61: How Can You Believe In God?

"Blessed is the man who makes the Lord his trust, who does not turn to the proud, to those who go astray after a lie." **Psalm 40:4 ESV**

Romanian born Eli Wiesel, a Jewish American professor and political activist as well as survivor of a Nazi death camp, was asked during an interview, "After all that has happened to you, how can you believe in God?" He responded, "After all that has happened to me how can I not believe in God!"

Is it surprising to you that in a bad world, bad things happen? Are you baffled when disasters occur in a world that is run by the master of disaster, Satan? Satan is the prince and the power of the air according to Scripture (**Ephesians 2:1-3**).

If you don't believe in God, you cannot see God. If you believe in God, you cannot help but see God in everything. *"Anyone who wants to come to him must believe that God exists and that he rewards those who sincerely seek him."* **Hebrews 11:6b NLT**

Because a person does not believe there is a God does not prove or suggest that He does not exist. May I suggest that a created one, a creation by the hand of the creator, does not possess the capacity to comprehend the slightest element of that which was not created but always existed, the Eternal One. Now I cannot go beyond this point, for it is a point of faith, and without faith you cannot come to God nor know God.

How can I believe in God, you may ask? I believe in God because I believe Him; I believe in His Word. That is it. I stand upon this simple but undeniable statement: I believe there is a God because I see Him in his Word. You cannot disprove that, and neither can anyone else, dead, alive or yet to be born. What I see, I see, though you see Him not.

I believe that Scripture is true because it is God's word. I believe God cannot lie, **Numbers 23:19 NLT** *"God is not a man, so he does not lie. He is not human, so he does not change his mind."* Why should there ever be a reason for one who knows all things to lie? God doesn't need to trick anyone. He is sovereign. That which He does, He does, and needs no reason for doing it.

I stand with Eli Wiesel: *"After all that has happened to me how can I not believe in God!"*

"Blessed is the man who makes the Lord his trust, who does not turn to the proud, to those who go astray after a lie!" **Psalm 40:4 ESV**

Think about it. *Selah!*

Day 62: The Expression Of A Mother's Work

"I remember your genuine faith, for you share the faith that first filled your grandmother Lois and your mother, Eunice." **2 Timothy 1:5 NLT**

Richard Hooker penned these words: *"Blessed forever and ever be that mother's child whose faith has made him the child of God. The earth may shake, the pillars of the world may tremble under us, the countenance of the heaven may be appalled, the sun may lose his light, the moon her beauty, the stars their glory; but concerning the man that trusts in God . . . what is there in this world that will change his heart, overthrow his faith, alter his affection towards God, or the affection of God to him?"*

Richard Hooker was a theologian and defender of the Church of England in the last part of the sixteenth century. My ancestors came to this new world in May of 1635. Rev. Tristram Thomas was Rector of Alfold Parish, County Surrey, and canon of Sundridge Church of Kent, England, at the time that Richard Hooker wrote these words and perhaps knew him.

By these words we can see the importance of what a mother can do for the good of all. Yet, if she fails to see her significance, a great blight can be brought upon this world. Hooker proclaims: *"I have a Shepherd full of kindness, full of care, and full of power; unto him I commit myself. His own finger has engraven this sentence in the tables of my heart, 'Satan has desired to winnow you as wheat, but I have prayed that your faith fail not.'*

Therefore the assurance of my hope I will labor to keep as a jewel unto the end; and by labor, through the gracious meditation of his prayer, I shall keep it."

Can you see his mother here? "Shepherd full of kindness; full of care, full of power; her own finger has engraven on his heart the things of God." Yes, his heart was shaped toward God through his mother's dedication, persistence, and faithfulness to him, her child.

I am thankful for my mother and her dedication, persistence, and faithfulness in raising my brother, my sisters, and me. She has engraved her love for God upon her grandchildren and great grandchildren that they may come to know this great Shepherd.

Think about it. *Selah!*

Day 63: Accepting The Things In Life.

"So humble yourselves under the mighty power of God, and at the right time he will lift you up in honor. Give all your worries and cares to God, for he cares about you. Stay alert! Watch out for your great enemy, the devil. He prowls around like a roaring lion, looking for someone to devour. Stand firm against him, and be strong in your faith. Remember that your family of believers all over the world is going through the same kind of suffering you are. In his kindness God called you to share in his eternal glory by means of Christ Jesus. So after you have suffered a little while, he will restore, support, and strengthen you, and he will place you on a firm foundation. All power to him forever! Amen." **1 Peter 5:6-11 NLT**

This is a long passage but one that must be read together. Everyone wants to live a happy and joyful life. Here are some important things that Peter points out which are necessary in serving Christ Jesus with joy:

1. Be humble; then you won't get as frustrated with those around you.

2. Give God your anxieties, and then you won't get in a hurry.

3. Checkout God's "beyond human" love for you, and you will never feel unappreciated or unloved.

4. Expect Satan to track you down and run you over just as he does all believers all

around the world, and then take action against him. Did you know that Satan hates you with the same hatred that he has for God?

5. Expect to suffer for Jesus and you will be amazed with the grace that God gives you. As you experience His grace, you will notice that you are glad and not mad, happy, and joyfully fulfilled in Christ Jesus.

6. You will feel restored, confirmed, strengthened, and well established as a believer.

Think about it. *Selah!*

Day 64: Famous Or Faithful?

"Who then is a faithful and wise servant, whom his master has set over his household, to give them their food at the proper time? Blessed is that servant whom his master will find so doing when he comes. Truly, I say to you, he will set him over all his possessions." **Matthew 24:45-47 ESV**

Don't seek high places in life; seek to be obedient and faithful. To be deemed faithful in the eyes of others brings glory to the one whom you are serving. That is God, and to Him belongs all the glory now and forever. To strive for personal fame brings you glory, but it will be a fleeting glory.

The congregation of believers in Corinth had a problem with wanting glory, but Paul informed them that their bodies were a temple of God and a place where God abides. They were not to think of themselves or their group as being prestigious, wise, or famous. They were servants of God just as all other believers are.

The Apostle Paul penned in **1 Corinthians 4:1-2**, *"This is how one should regard us, as servants of Christ and stewards of the mysteries of God. Moreover, it is required of stewards that they be found faithful."* **ESV**

In **The Message**, Eugene Peterson paraphrases this verse: *"Don't imagine us leaders to be something we aren't. We are servants of Christ, not his masters. We are guides into God's most sublime secrets, not security*

guards posted to protect them. The requirements for a good guide are reliability and accurate knowledge. It matters very little what you think of me, even less where I rank in popular opinion. I don't even rank myself."

The point here is, don't strive to be noticed, but strive to be faithful to God's assignment that He has given you. Strive to be reliable in your word, to be accurate in your understanding of God's Word, to be consistent and dependable in your living, and to be consistent in your love for God and your love for others. We are required by God to be found faithful at all times.

What about your life? What is your aim in life? Do you do things to be famous or to be faithful?

Think about it. *Selah!*

Day 65: Worthy Of Worship

"You shall have no other gods before me. You shall not make for yourself a carved image, or any likeness of anything that is in heaven above, or that is in the earth beneath, or that is in the water under the earth. You shall not bow down to them or serve them, for I the Lord your God am a jealous God, visiting the iniquity of the fathers on the children to the third and fourth generation of those who hate me, but showing steadfast love to thousands of those who love me and keep my commandments." **Exodus 20:3-6 ESV**

Why would anyone want to worship "another god"? Another god other than the One who just *"brought you out"* of an oppressive land, who single-handedly delivered you by the might of His hand alone and snatched you out of the clutches of slavery?

The top item on the top-ten list of "don't" is idol worship. Why would this nation want to be like the defeated people, the ones who have been conquered, whose gods were all exposed as fake and helpless?

Why? It seems hard to understand, but it happened quickly to this people. The first thing they did was murmur, grumble, and complain to the "One God," to Him who was and is and is to come, to the I AM, Jehovah God. Why?

They seemed to have a personal idea about God and about worship that seemed to be right but not worship that was right. Joni Eareckson Tada writes with Steven

Estes in the book, **When God Weeps**, as it was with "*Normal* countries—Israel began mumbling—had less demanding gods, visible ones you could see and know were there and could carve into a shape that suited you. Their worship services ended with dessert, pleasure on the heels of prayer, brotherly-sisterly fellowship with those lovely priests and priestesses who tended so well to the worshiper's libidino- [lustful, lewd, carnal, libertine, depraved, decadent and promiscuous] spiritual needs."

That is idol worship. It is not the worship of **Revelation 4:8-11 ESV:** *"Holy, holy, holy is the Lord God almighty . . . Worthy are you, our Lord and God, to receive glory and honor and power . . . . "* Idol worship is preferred worship. It is custom-made worship. It is worship that makes us feel good; worship that speaks to us, not to God. Isn't God the One to whom all worship is worthy, to Him alone?

Worship must be a free expression to God of His worthiness of praise and honor. Worship must be glorious to God; it must make Him feel glorious. The worshipper is not the key. It is He to whom the worship is directed.

May I ask a key question? Have you carved an image of worship that you like? Can you worship with other believers who are genuinely offering genuine praise and worship to the One and only God? Do you complain and murmur at others who are worshiping the One God? If so, you may want to re-evaluate why you are worshiping and to whom your worship is directed.

There is a lot of discussion about "worship wars" today, but if you are involved in that war, you cannot be worshipping. There is no war in worship. We read in **James 4:1 NLT**, *"What is causing the quarrels and fights among you? Don't they come from the evil desires at war within you?"*

Think about it. *Selah!*

Day 66: Bearing Each Other's Burdens

"Bear one another's burdens, and so fulfill the law of Christ. For if anyone thinks he is something, when he is nothing, he deceives himself." **Galatians 6:2-3 ESV**

I don't know about you but I have a problem with not sharing with others the difficulties that I may be facing. I guess the reason is that I don't want to be a burden or place a concern upon them. I have the idea that I may be causing them to worry and they have enough to worry about. I am also slow to share a blessing that God has done for me because I think others may think I am bragging. I am inclined to feel that I want to do things for others but that I am sufficient to care for myself.

My wife has taken me to the woodshed on this matter. She informed me that she cares about me and so does my family and church. She made me aware that I was not allowing the believers around me to bear my burdens and share in the blessings and, therefore, I was a stumbling block to them in doing what Jesus commanded us to do. I was thinking that I was something that I wasn't.

She is right and I am wrong. Now, saying I am wrong is very difficult for me. It is especially difficult to put it into print; but here it is because this is a serious error and sin on my part. Yes, we do need to share our lives with other believers, friends, and loved ones. Yes, we ought to honor and magnify God, and I, in particular, need to reveal to others His good hand upon my life by bragging about what He has done for me. This is encouraging and fulfilling to others.

The Christian life is not one that needs to be hidden, but exposed and held high and lighted for all to see. *"You are the light of the world. A city set on a hill cannot be hidden. Nor do people light a lamp and put it under a basket, but on a stand, and it gives light to all in the house. In the same way, let your light shine before others, so that they may see your good works and give glory to your Father who is in heaven."*
Matthew 5:14-16 ESV

Allow others to pray with you about things. Allow them to share in the joys of your life and let them follow the command of Jesus. I am going to make an assertive effort to overcome this fault in my life. So would you pray with me about this shortcoming?

Think about it. *Selah!*

Day 67: Would You Still Say God Is Good?

"If you need wisdom, ask our generous God, and he will give it to you. He will not rebuke you for asking. But when you ask him, be sure that your faith is in God alone. Do not waver, for a person with divided loyalty is as unsettled as a wave of the sea that is blown and tossed by the wind. Such people should not expect to receive anything from the Lord. Their loyalty is divided between God and the world, and they are unstable in everything they do." **James 1:5-8 NLT**

I recently read this note by a young lady I know: *"Would you still say God is good if He doesn't answer your prayer the way you want Him to? I hope I do."* That caused me to evaluate my prayer life.

George Mueller, the great man of prayer and faith, wrote: *"Concerning everything we have to pray. Not simply when great troubles come, when our house in on fire, or our beloved wife is at the point of death, or our dear children are laid down in sickness, not simply at such times, but also in little things. From the very early morning, let us make everything a matter of prayer, and let it be so throughout the day, and throughout our whole life."* We need to pray for our own well being as a follower of Christ. We should ask Him and ask in faith.

Did you know that God always answers our prayers and always goes way beyond what we might be expecting Him to do? God's plan for us and His assignment for us, is always up-to-date and is always for our good. God's vision is much better than ours, and His plan is far beyond our expectations and desires.

There is never a time when you have sincerely prayed to God that He does not respond appropriately, proficiently, and on time, that is, with His perfect "timing." Our problem is that we expect Him to respond as we wish, not as He knows best. We often are telling God what we want Him to do rather that asking Him what is best for us to do. We want "our will" done in heaven as we want it done on earth.

"Would you still say God is good if He doesn't answer your prayer the way you want Him to? I hope I do." The question proposed is a valid one that each of us needs to consider as we do the assignment that God has given us. It is true that we can do all things through Christ Jesus our Lord and that He will supply all that we need and way above all that we might ask or even think **(Philippians 4:13,19; Ephesians 3:20)**; but we must seek His lead, His road, His path, and His way. He is God, and we are not.

Think about it. *Selah!*

Day: 68: Yes, God Shall Supply It All

"Jesus Christ is the same yesterday and today and forever." **Hebrews 13:8 ESV**

Jesus never fails. Jesus can be trusted on the basis of His sufficiency in the past. If He met your need then, He will meet it today, and He will meet it tomorrow as well. The only problem a believer may have is his patience for today. If we pray, God will hear and if we have a great need, He will meet that need. We must only trust Him.

In the "Model Prayer" there is this line: *"Give us this day our daily bread"* (**Matthew 6:9**). It is a prayer for God to meet our need of substance and was a model that Jesus himself issued.

Perhaps the best-known story of George Mueller is the following:

> One morning at the orphanage, George had the table to be set for breakfast, but there was no food or milk. The children sat waiting for their daily bread. A knock sounded at the door. It was the baker. "Mr. Mueller," he said, "I couldn't sleep last night. Somehow I felt you didn't have bread for breakfast, so I got up at 2:00 AM and baked some fresh bread." A second knock sounded. The milkman had broken down right in front of the orphanage, and he wanted to give the children his milk so he could empty his wagon and repair it.

Were these coincidences? I don't think so. It was the good hand of God doing what He said He would. *"Jesus, Christ is the same yesterday and today and forever"* (**Hebrews 13:8 ESV**). If He met your need in the past, He will meet it now and in the future. He does not change.

No, these were not coincidences. You see, at 2:00 o'clock in the morning, God summoned a baker to have the bread prepared for the orphanage's breakfast. There was no need for George to be worried that night for God had already caused a baker to start baking and arranged for a milkman to have the milk on hand and ready to deliver. George's responsibility was to trust, and trust he did.

So this same Jesus who met the needs of the children at the orphanage in England in the late 1800's and early 1900's will meet your need in the same way in these present days of the 2000's.

So ask, trust, wait, and be happy and confident that Jesus never changes His mind. He is always the same.

Think about it. *Selah!*

Day 69: Never Fear Doing What God Gives You To Do

"What time I am afraid, I will trust in thee." **Psalm 56:3 KJV**

Psalm 56:3 is one of my wife's favorite verses that she memorized as a child. Her brother, Clifford, was a paratrooper in the 82nd Airborne Division and a chaplain's assistant during the Korean War. His job was to protect the chaplain as they jumped behind enemy lines. He protected the chaplain because chaplains not carry a gun. When he came home after the war, he had a Samurai sword. The knowledge that her brother was in the house and that he had that sword made my wife feel safe and unafraid during the night as a child. When he was not at home or at times when fear would creep into her mind, she would quote, *"What time I am afraid I will trust in thee."*

I'm sure you are aware of this fact that fear is not limited to the lives of children. It invades the lives of adults also. Fear is a product of doubt and uncertainty. Fear comes to believers and non-believers alike, but it has no place in the life of a believer because God is our help, God is our strength, and God is our protector. His sword is the sword of His mouth, or His word. David writes in **Psalm 27:1 & 3:** *"The Lord is the stronghold of my life; of whom shall I be afraid? . . . Though an army encamp against me, my heart shall not fear; though war arise against me, yet I will be confident."*

Though we may be dropped behind enemy lines and within their stronghold, there is no cause to be afraid for it is God who has placed us there. Where God is, there can be no fear. Where God is there can be no doubt or lack of confidence. God's Word is sure, His plan is sure, and His people can be assured of success. If it is God who called us, ". . . *who can be against us?"* **Romans 8:31 KJV**

So, are you a believer? Has God given you an assignment? Has He called you to do that assignment? If the answer to those questions is yes, then you have no cause for fear. What can man do to you?

In whom have you placed your trust? There is no need to spend your nights in sleeplessness, for God is your comfort and He has sent The Comforter to bring you comfort. God has supplied you with all you need. He knows the future so you will not lack anything. Draw near to God, rest in God's Word, trust in His promises, and be confident and happy in doing what He has assigned. **James 4:7 ESV** tells us: *"Resist the Devil and he will flee from you."*

Sleep in the arms of God, listen to His song of comfort that He is singing in your ear and the Devil will take a hike. *"What time I am afraid, I will trust in thee,"* **Psalm 56:3 KJV.**

Think about it. *Selah!*

Day 70: My Strength And My Redeemer

"Let the words of my mouth and the meditation of my heart be acceptable in your sight, O Lord, my strength and my redeemer." **Psalm 19:14 NKJV**

Every morning, as I pray to the Lord during my daily devotion and quiet time with Him, I recite **Psalm 14:19**. I want every word that I say and every thought that I think during the day to be pleasing and acceptable to my Lord Jesus Christ who is my strength and who has redeemed me. Those last seven words are wonderful, are they not?   Because of them we can face the challenges of the day *(my strength)* and not worry about the failures that we make throughout the day *(my redeemer)*.   Think about those two words: *strength, redeemer.*

What is it about the words that we say that need constant evaluation? When we are critical, the reason is that we think we can do those things better. It also may be that we think we should be in charge, or we do not want to be challenged. We think we are stronger and more knowledgeable than others. We might say, "*Who do they think they are? I could have done a better job. Why wasn't I asked?*" Those words are not acceptable in God's sight. Those thoughts are not pleasing to God and profitable for the advancement of His message. I guess we want everyone else to be acceptable in our sight.

God is our strength, so we should act and do in His strength not our own. God is our redeemer, so we should understand that we have failed and are in need of a redeemer. If we have these thoughts in our mind throughout the day, we are not as likely to lord ourselves over others and gloat in their failure or in their missing the desired mark.

If we consider weakness, and understand that all our accomplishments and successes are because of and through the strength of our Redeemer, we then come to the understanding that we have nothing to complain about. If we understand that we can do nothing in and of ourselves, and the things that we attempt to do, in and of ourselves, fall far short of the perfection that God expects, we are less likely to revel in the shortcomings of others.

We want to be encouragers and fellow laborers with them. We are all one body, aren't we? *"For just as the body is one and has many members, and all the members of the body, though many, are one body, so it is with Christ,"* **1 Corinthians 12:12 ESV.** *"Let no one deceive himself. If anyone among you thinks that he is wise in this age, let him become a fool that he may become wise,"* **1 Corinthians 3:18 ESV.**

The truth is, people judge us by our words and deeds. The words that we say come from the thoughts that we have been meditating on, and those thoughts and words then shape the person we really are. Therefore, we come to understand that we need strength to be a follower of Christ, and we need redemption, not only from our past sins but also from our many failures throughout the day.

Jesus is faithful and just to forgive us our sin of criticism and can purify our thoughts throughout the day if we trust in Him and focus on Him.

Draw near to God, and He will draw near to you; and your thoughts will be of Him, our strength and our Redeemer. **James 4:7-8; Psalm 19:14**

Think about it, *Selah!*

Day 71: What Do You Do If You Just Don't Have What It Takes?

"God saved you by his grace when you believed. And you can't take credit for this; it is a gift from God. Salvation is not a reward for the good things we have done, so none of us can boast about it. For we are God's masterpiece. He has created us anew in Christ Jesus, so we can do the good things he planned for us long ago."
Ephesians 2:8-10 NLT

Have you ever started something that you thought you could do but after you got into the project you soon discovered that you just didn't have what it takes to complete it? I have many times. Just the other day, my wife asked me to replace a light socket in a lamp. It seemed to be something I thought I could do. I took the lamp apart, removed the light socket, took it with me to a building supply store, and bought a replacement socket just like the one I removed. When I returned home, I put it all together, three times, in that I forgot that there was an order I needed to follow. Having successfully done that, I reassembled the lamp, put in the bulb, plugged up the lamp and turned the switch. Pop! The circuit switch was tripped, so I unplugged the lamp and again reassembled the socket—much faster, I might add, than my first three attempts. I then plugged up the lamp, turned on the switch and POP! The circuit switch tripped. Three more times I went through the process and each time with the same results. I then went upstairs and brought down another lamp for my wife. I discovered something was wrong, but I didn't know what it was. I just didn't have what it took to do such a simple task.

I'm fairly confident that everyone has found himself or herself in some type of situation where they discovered that they needed help.

Eternal life is a gift that cannot be achieved and Heaven is a destination that cannot be reached by any person that has ever been born on this earth with the one exception of Jesus Christ, God's Son, a gift to the world. No one can be good enough to receive and reach these. No one can because no one is righteous. *"There is none righteous, no not one,"* the Bible tells us, **Romans 3:10-12**. We are all as lost sheep who have gone astray and beyond help, **Isaiah 53:6.** But thanks be to God for His precious Son Jesus Christ who is capable and has what it takes to achieve each of these goals. It is free and is offered to all without exception. All that is needed is to take Jesus Christ as your Savior, **John 3:16-18.**

So, because we don't have what it takes, the only one who does have what it takes has taken the steps to make it possible for you to do what you are incapable of doing on your own.

Why not take Him up on His offer? Pray to Him and say: *"Lord Jesus, I am a sinner. I know I cannot go to heaven on my own and that there is no other way to get to heaven except through you. I believe that you are the very Son of the Living God. I believe that you came to earth for the very purpose of doing what I cannot do. I*

believe that you died for my sin debt. I believe that you rose from the grave and that you are right now in heaven preparing a place for your followers. I know that you will come again one day to take those believers with you to heaven, and I want to be one of them. So, I confess my sins before you, and I ask that you forgive me for my sins of the past, for today, and for the rest of my life. I take you as my Lord and Savior right now.

Thank you! I will seek to do your will and follow you in your strength and not in my own. Help me to keep my eyes on you and off the world. Help me to make disciples for you all the days of my life from this day forward. Amen."

If you sincerely did this, you are a new creation, not because of the deeds, but because of your faith in Christ.

Think about it. *Selah!*

Day 72: How Often Does God Think About You?

"The Lord directs the steps of the godly. He delights in every detail of their lives." **Psalm 37:23 NLT**

Have you ever wondered how often you are on the mind of God? Is there ever a time that He is unaware of where you are, what you are doing, what your needs are at the moment, and what is on your mind? The answer is no, there is never a millisecond of your whole life that God is not fully aware and totally prepared for.

"For the strength of the wicked will be shattered, but the Lord takes care of the godly. Day by day the Lord takes care of the innocent, and they will receive an inheritance that lasts forever. They will not be disgraced in hard times; even in famine they will have more than enough. But the wicked will die. The Lord's enemies are like flowers in a field—they will disappear like smoke." **Psalm 37:17-20 NLT**

God takes care of the godly and the innocent are in the hands of the Lord. In **Psalm 139:1 NLT,** David acknowledges: *"O Lord, you have examined my heart and know everything about me."* In **Psalm 138,** David sings God's praise because of the knowledge of God's unfailing love, faithfulness, and care for him, and the comfort that he has in God by knowing that God's promises are backed up by the honor of His name. He is encouraged by the thought that God hears and answers every prayer that he prays.

How much does God care about you and how often are you on his mind? He cares with unfailing love. He knows every thought and need that you have at all times, moment-by-moment, day by day, and throughout all the years of your life. God has you on His mind, and you are within His view. The good times are from His hand. In the bad times, He takes your hand. In all the in-between times, He strengthens your hand. He is ever with you and always around you.

This does not mean that all things are good that happen to you, because you live in a wicked world that has Satan as its prince; but know that this evil prince has already been overcome and is awaiting his sentence to be enacted. God loves you and cares for you throughout the bad times. Remember, this is not heaven; we're not there yet. So hold on to God's unchanging and all sufficient hand and rest in His arms.

Jesus loved Lazarus but He waited to let him die that the glory of God might be seen in a greater way. We see His love in **John 11:33-36 NLT:** *"When Jesus saw her weeping and saw the other people wailing with her, he was moved with indignation and was deeply troubled. 'Where have you put him?' he asked them. They told him, 'Lord, come and see.' Then Jesus wept. The people who were standing nearby said, 'See how much he love him!' "*

He loves you with that same passion. Yes, you are on God's mind right now, and His thoughts of you will never come to an end.

Think about it. *Selah!*

Day 73: Does Death Frighten You?

"Yea, though I walk through the valley of the shadow of death, I will fear no evil: for thou art with me." **Psalm 23:4 KJV**

Does the thought of death frighten you? I would say that the thought of death, for the overwhelming majority of people, is a fearful thing. Death is a fearful thought because we know nothing about what is on the other side of death. For a human being there is only speculation. The only knowledge we have is that which others have speculated. There is one **exception** and that is Jesus Christ. Jesus Christ conquered death and the grave. Having done that, He tells those of us who are believers, those of us who have faith in Him, that we need not fear. (**I Corinthians 15:54-58**)

Psalm 23 is a Scripture that is read many times at the burial of believers in Christ Jesus. May I take just one verse out of that chapter and let us think about it. *"Yea, though I walk through the valley of the shadow of death, I will fear no evil: for thou art with me"* (**Psalm 23:4 KJV**). Let me put it in my own words: God is with us and He has promised to never leave us, and He has promised to never to fail us. This is a promise of God to believers. Because He is faithful and cannot lie, whatever He says we can count on and never have a second thought about it other than what He says is the truth, the "Gospel Truth."

Now with that understanding of God and His word, let us take a look at this sentence in **Psalm 23**. There is never a reason for me to fear in this short, temporary, and uncertain life on earth. The only certain thing is Truth, and Truth is God, and God alone is Truth. Any statement aside from God is not the truth, so it is a lie. If something is almost the truth, this makes it a total lie. Just a hint of a lie is a complete lie. So here is the truth, *"And as it is appointed unto men once to die, but after this the judgment."* **Hebrews 9:27 KJV**

Everyone will die and everyone will face God, whether they chose to believe it or not. It is a fearful thing to stand before a living God (**Hebrews 10:31**). This is where fear comes in, but this fear is only for those who do not believe in God. The believer has no need to fear for we have the peace of Christ within us and the righteousness of Christ upon us. (**2 Corinthians 5:21**)

Now that is the background for this sentence. Jesus is with us always. He will never leave us and even when we have to die, He is with us. Death is the last hurdle for the human being, and when we go over it, Jesus is right there with us. He has already been through it and conquered it. Now we can trust Him through the whole appointment of death, and we can have peace in the face of death because of the presence of Jesus. Nothing can happen to us without Jesus' presence. So, have no fear, He is there. The shadow is what we fear because the shadow is the unknown; but the shadow cannot hurt anyone. Jesus stands with us, overshadowing death, because He is the Light behind the shadow, and He is our peace.

Think about it. *Selah!*

Day 74: Monkey See, Monkey Do.

"You shall love the Lord your God with all your heart and with all your soul and with all your might. And these words that I command you today shall be on your heart. You shall teach them diligently to your children, and shall talk of them when you sit in your house, and when you walk by the way, and when you lie down, and when you rise. You shall bind them as a sign on your hand, and they shall be as frontlets between your eyes. You shall write them on the doorposts of your house and on your gates."
Deuteronomy 6:5-9 ESV

Solomon encouraged his son to hear the instructions and teachings of his father and mother because they would prove to be of great value and a shining pendant to all those whom he might come in contact with throughout all his life. How you act, what you do, what you say, and your consistent conduct in life will speak volumes loudly to everyone.

Your conduct in life's situations reveals who you really are. No one needs to be informed about you, they observe you.

Where do you get your values? You get them from those individuals that catch your eye as you grow. Solomon encouraged his children to pay attention to his instructions and not to ignore the values that their mother taught (**Proverbs 1:8-9**). His children's problem was that what they saw in the lives of their father and mother contradicted what they heard. The truths taught were valuable but were questioned because of how Solomon and his many wives conducted themselves in their daily lives.

This is what God instructed Moses to teach the children of Israel: Hear, teach, and demonstrate by your actions in your daily life. It is true that "truths are not taught, they are caught." Children are more inclined to do what they "see" others do than what they are told by others to do. It is like the old adage: "monkey see, monkey do." Be careful how you react to insults in life. Be cautious of your actions in response to the actions of others. Harness your words; be thoughtful and aware of those little ears around you. Remember that *"little ears have big mouths,"* or as I have heard someone say, *"What should not be heard by little ears, should not be said by big mouths."*

God's instructions to Moses for parents could have changed the direction of the future of the children of Israel, but those instructions went unheeded. As a result, the parents died in the wilderness. It wasn't long until there arose a generation that knew not God because they did not hear about what God had done for them and their family, and they did not see a commitment to God before them by their parents. The children did not see God in the daily lives of their parents (**Judges 2:10**). The result was that the children turned to other gods they saw in the lives of others.

What about you? It is not too late. Be an example to your children and grandchildren; and don't stop there. Be an example of the good hand of God and the glory of God to all those, both great and small, in your daily life.

Let them see Christ in you and do as Jesus told us: "Go and make disciples, now!"

Think about it. *Selah!*

Day 75: Mountains And Valleys

"The voice of him that crieth in the wilderness, Prepare ye the way of the Lord, make straight in the desert a highway for our God. Every valley shall be exalted, and every mountain and hill shall be made low: and the crooked shall be made straight, and the rough places plain. **Isaiah 40:3-4 KJV**

In 1741, George Frideric Handel composed his famous oratorio, *The Messiah.* The scriptures were complied by Charles Jennens (a landowner, patron of the arts, and man of deep knowledge of the Bible) from the **King James Bible** and the *Psalms* that were included in the *Book of Common Prayer.*

The Air for Tenor, "Every Valley," is one of my favorites, perhaps for the fact that life is made up of mountains and valleys. Those mountains and valleys and the rough places in the road of life cause us much stress, fear, doubt, and uncertainty about our future. We spend much time worrying and fretting over those mountains and valleys, those rough places before us. I might add here that they are unnecessary moments of fear, doubt, and question for the believer.

This great passage is placed before us as a comfort. **Isaiah 40** begins with *"Comfort ye, comfort ye my people, saith your God."* Think about this: God Himself is telling Isaiah to comfort the followers of God. Valleys are merely moments of exaltation for our God. Mountains in our eyes are made low before Him, and there are no curves in the road or the path that He has prepared for us.

What we see before us is an opportunity to personally feel His great love. God loves us, and before we were even born He made the provisions that were needed for our mountains, valleys, and rough places. All things are clear before our great God.

So, say to your mountain, "Be cast into the sea!" Say to your storm, "Be still!" Fill in that valley with the glory of God and watch it rise up in praise to our God. Nothing surprises God, nothing hinders Him, and all things are used by Him for His glory.

Think about it. *Selah!*

Day 76: "God Is Who He Is And Cannot Be Any *Is-er*"

"God said to Moses, 'I AM Who I AM'. And he said, 'Say this to the people of Israel, 'I AM has sent me to you.' " **Exodus 3:14 ESV**

My Father-in-Law used to say this, "God is God and He can't be any *is-er*." We would laugh, but the truth is God is God, and there is no other God beside Him. There cannot be any other true God, there can only be one.

This was what God was telling Moses here in **Exodus 3:14.** The God that "IS," is the God who has sent Moses to the people of Israel enslaved in Egypt. The "I AM" God is and cannot be anything else. He is faithful and cannot be unfaithful. He is love and cannot be unloving. He is sufficient for all things and cannot fall short. He is just and cannot be unjust in anything. He is holy and cannot be unholy, impure, or tainted in any way. He always has been and always will be and cannot be a memory. God is, "I AM," He says. He is the eternal now, the eternal day. He is light and in Him is no darkness. He is consistent, sure, and constant in all that He wills, and there is not even a hint or shadow of turning. *"Every good gift and every perfect gift is from above, coming down from the Father of lights with whom there is no variation or shadow due to change."* **James 1:17 ESV**

"Yes, *God is how He is and cannot be any is-er.*" So what is your concern for today? Have you asked God about it? I want you to know that He has heard your request, and He has already put into action what is the best way to answer that request. Trust Him, wait on Him and let Him work out His plan in your life. He is faithful and cannot be anything less. Don't worry! God is listening.

Think about it. *Selah!*

Day 77: Why Doesn't God Do Something?

"The Lord is slow to anger and great in power, and the Lord will by no means clear the guilty." **Nahum 1:3 ESV**

It is hard to look about this earth and see the great atrocities that seem to flourish and not wonder why God does not do something about them. Christians are persecuted in great numbers with a vow to eradicate them from the face of the earth and the Jews as well. It seems as though the nations are OK with it. We see no real effort made to slow it down or stop it, and we pray for deliverance. Where is God?

We can read many times in Scripture where revenge from the hand of God is requested against great suffering. We read in **Habakkuk 1:2 ESV,** *"O Lord, how long shall I cry for help, and you will not hear?"*

The answer is this: God does hear. God is acting but He does things in His own time and not ours. **Nahum 1:3** says, *"The Lord is slow to anger . . . ."* In **2 Peter 3:9 ESV** we find, *"The Lord is . . . patient toward you, not wishing that any should perish, but that all should reach repentance."* Jonah was not patient. Humanity in general and you and I in particular do not possess the patience of God. We may have the patience of Job, but Job's patience was insufficient.

We must understand that God has already acted against the violence and the acts of Satan against us. God's actions were pronounced at the cross and with the resurrection of His only begotten Son, Jesus. Now is the time we must stand firm and stand in patience for the tribulation in view. What we see today is not the end. Sin is not winning and Satan is not in control, but God is. What God is doing we may find difficult to understand, but we don't have to understand the plan. We just need to trust the Planner.

We must understand that every Christian will have to suffer from time to time, and we must expect it as Jesus did. **2 Timothy 3:12 NLT** says, *"Yes, and everyone who wants to live a godly life in Christ Jesus will suffer persecution."*

Romans 8:17 NLT: *"And since we are his children, we are his heirs. In fact, together with Christ we are heirs of God's glory. But if we are to share his glory, we must also share his suffering."*

John 15:20 NLT: *"Do you remember what I told you? 'A slave is not greater than the master.' Since they persecuted me, naturally they will persecute you. And if they had listened to me, they would listen to you."*

Why doesn't God do something? The answer is that He already has but He is patient and wants everyone to have all the time necessary to repent and turn to Him. He has asked that you and I go and tell the world about His Good News. So, the real question is to you and to me. Why aren't you doing that which He has called you to do, and why haven't I done what He has asked? The question is, why haven't I?

Think about it. *Selah!*

Day 78: Ambassadors Not Citizens

"for which I am an ambassador in chains; that in it I may speak boldly, as I ought to speak." **Ephesians 6:20 NKJV**

"We are Christ's ambassadors; God is making his appeal through us . . ."
2 Corinthians 5:20 NLT

Jesus told his disciples that the world would hate them because they were His followers and that this world was not their home. Paul tells us that we are not citizens of this world but our citizenship is in heaven. *"For our citizenship is in heaven, from which we also eagerly wait for the Savior, the Lord Jesus Christ, who will transform our lowly body that it may be conformed to His glorious body according to the working by which He is able even to subdue all things to Himself."* **Philippians 3:20-21 NKJV**

We are in this world as the ambassadors of Jesus, and we are here to represent Him with the offer of eternal life to whosoever would believe. We are strangers and wayfarers and just passing through on our way to our new home in heaven.

While here we are not to be conformed to this world and other religions or the thought processes and philosophies of academia. We are to be transformed in our thinking to the mind of Christ (**Romans 12:2**). We aren't supposed to think like the world, act like the world, or be assimilated into this world. We are to teach reformation to Christ, not conformation to the world.

We won't be here long, only as long as our assignment is. We will soon be called home or taken to our new home that Jesus is preparing for us. *"For we know that when this earthly tent we live in is taken down (that is, when we die and leave this earthly body), we will have a house in heaven, an eternal body made for us by God himself and not by human hands."* **2 Corinthians 5:1 NLT**

Until that time comes, be a good ambassador.

Think about it. *Selah!*

Day 79: There's No Place Like Home

"Then Christ will make his home in your hearts as you trust in him. Your roots will grow down into God's love and keep you strong. **Ephesians 3:17 NLT**

People everywhere love to sing songs about home, songs that cause us to reminisce of our early days at home. We sing songs like, "There's No Place Like Home," "Home For The Holidays," and "Home on the Range." Those are just a few of the old ones from the past. We enjoy using phrases like, "If you're not at home, you should be," "I just feel at home here," or "Homeboy," etc. The truth is that the thought of home brings comfort, love, and freedom to us. There is no fear at home, and we find great strength at home. We feel empowered at home.

When we leave home, we say we are going to "Lay down roots of our own, start a new family, or build a home." That is what Jesus is doing for believers right now. He told His disciples that He was going away to prepare a new home for them and us. He said that when everything was just right, He would be back to take us to that new home (**John 14:2-3**). In the meantime, our bodies are the home of Jesus. Jesus wants to feel at home in our lives just as much as we want to feel at home anywhere else. No one enjoys being at a place where they do not feel at home, and the same is true with Jesus. Followers of Jesus ought to follow Him, obey Him and live a life that makes Him feel at home.

Our challenge is to be a reflection of Christ Jesus to the world in such a way that the people of this world will want to have the same peace and contentment that we have with Jesus in our lives.

So, what about you—do you have a life that is comforting to Jesus? Do other believers feel at home around you? If not, perhaps there is some housekeeping that needs to be done in your life. My prayer for you is that Jesus will feel more and more at home in your life.

Think about it. *Selah!*

Day 80: God Doesn't Make Puppets

"The Lord is good, a strong refuge when trouble comes. He is close to those who trust in him. But he will sweep away his enemies in an overwhelming flood. He will pursue his foes into the darkness of night. Why are you scheming against the Lord? He will destroy you with one blow; he won't need to strike twice!" **Nahum 1:7-9 NLT**

People create puppets. God creates people. People make puppets do as they wish, and the puppet has no will of its own. God created people with a personal will and with the ability to do as they wish, but God knows the decisions and choices that His creations will make on their own.

Puppets seem to be real in the hand of a gifted puppeteer, but they are not real. We are amazed by the skill of the puppeteer with his puppet or the ventriloquist's dummy. They seem so real but they are not. People are real but sometimes seem to act in an unreal manner.

The puppeteer or ventriloquist receives the glory for his creation. God receives the glory for his creations now or later. God receives glory by those who choose to obey Him and serve Him now; but those who choose to disobey Him now will bow before him at the Great White Throne Judgment and God will be glorified then.

Way before the earth was created, God knew by name exactly who would choose Him and who would refuse Him. God is long-suffering, and He waits because of His great love for all His creation. He does not want anyone to perish.

Yes, God is patient. He is kind and He is loving; but He is also righteously jealous and full of total vengeance, fury, and wrath. It is a fearful thing to stand before an angry and holy God.

So what is your choice? Whom do you choose to serve? Puppets and dummies have no future, but people do. They will live forever with Christ, or they will experience eternal death. The choice is yours.

To this you might say, "I don't believe any of that, I don't even believe in God, heaven or hell." Well, the choice is yours and you may not believe, but what if you are wrong? What if you are dead wrong?

Think about it. *Selah!*

Day 81: The Real You

"But the Lord said to Samuel, 'Do not look on his appearance or on the height of his stature, because I have rejected him. For the Lord sees not as man sees: man looks on the outward appearance, but the Lord looks on the heart." **1 Samuel 16:6-7 ESV**

Dr. Ben Carson, Presidential candidate for the 2016 election, had this to say in response to the question regarding race:

> "You know, I was asked once by a NPR reporter why I don't talk about race that often. And I said it's because I'm a neurosurgeon. And she looked at me quite quizzically. And I said, you see, when I take someone to the operating room and I peel down the scalp and take off the bone flap and open the dura, I'm operating on the thing that makes the person who they are. It's not the covering, the skin color, or the hair, that makes them who they are. We need to be looking for things that we can take out of this situation that will be helpful, not things that inflame the situation. Let's tone down the rhetoric and recognize that we, the people, are not each other's enemies."

In **1 Samuel 16,** the Lord God instructs the prophet-priest Samuel not to make a decision based upon how a person looks, but to look at the real person, the heart of the person. The heart is the real person. We often use phrases such as, *getting to the heart of the matter;*

talking from the heart, and he has a good heart, to point out an honest person or an honest and dependable statement.

Here is the truth: You cannot fool God, He knows your heart, He knows the real you, and He sees you as you actually are. When we pray and when we make commitments or statements, God sees right through them. He sees all the way to your heart, the real you.

So, what I am saying is:
1. Be honest to God. He knows the real you.
2. Be honest to yourself. You should know better and God can guide you.
3. Don't be fooled by Satan's wiles. He can fool you.
4. God knows best. Seek Him and follow Him.

Did you know that the wiles or schemes of the Devil are active, alive, and at work in your life daily? You must learn to recognize those schemes. They are as old as the earth and can be summed up as: the pride of life, the desires of the flesh, the desires of the eyes, and the pride of possessions (**1 John 2:15-17**). Our desires and our pride must be in line with God's heart and His will.

James 1:16 warns us not to be deceived by the things of life but to ask God for guidance and judge things from a spiritual eye. In **James 4:7-8** we see the secret and that is to resist the wiles of the devil and to draw near to God.

God knows the real you.

Think about it. *Selah!*

Day 82: Given To Change

"I am the Lord, and I do not change. That is why you descendants of Jacob are not already destroyed." **Malachi 3:6 NLT**

"The times they are a changin'," wrote Bob Dylan in the early 60's. *"The present now will later be past . . . ."* Why does time change? It changes because it will soon end and what follows time is eternity. Time by its own design is to measure a beginning and an end. What begins will end. This is where God comes into view because He has always been and He will never end. God operates outside the walls of time. *"A day is the same as a thousand years and a thousand years is of the same"* **2 Peter 3:8 ESV** *"But do not overlook this one fact, beloved, that with the Lord one day is as a thousand years, and a thousand years as or day."*

Malachi reminded Israel of the fact that he has no need to change. *"I am the Lord, and I do not change. That is why you descendants of Jacob are not already destroyed."* **Malachi 3:6 NLT**

Nations change, politicians change, churches change, terrain changes, environments change, and everything that is subject to time changes but God does not change. God is not affected by the opinion of change because He does not change and has no need for change. He is all knowing and there is nothing new in the boundaries of time that He is not well familiar with.

This brings me to the truth here: When we pray, when we bring our concerns to God, understand that He is well aware of our concerns, and He knows exactly why He allowed them to come about and how they will end and when they will end. Therefore, we must pray, make our requests to God, and bring our praises to God. Having done that, leave it there before God who does not change but who cares greatly for us. *"Give all your worries and cares to God, for he cares about you."*
1 Peter 5:7 NLT

Think about it. *Selah!*

Day 83: Draw Near To God

"Submit yourselves therefore to God. Resist the devil, and he will flee from you. Draw near to God, and he will draw near to you." **James 4:7-8 ESV**

Anselm of Canterbury was the Archbishop of Canterbury from 1093 through 1109. Anselm's writings on Scripture and on the importance of faith in knowing God and obtaining true knowledge have been widely read by scholars through the centuries. He stressed the supreme importance of one being quiet before God as necessary for the believer to come to a clear understanding of Scripture, in exercising our faith, and in knowing God rightly.

He wrote this:

> *"Up now, slight man! Flee for a little while thy occupations; hide thyself from these disturbing thoughts. Cast aside now thy burdensome cares, and put away thy toilsome business. Yield room for some little time with God, and rest for some little time with Him. Enter the inner chamber of thy mind; shut out all thoughts save that of God and such as can aid thee in seeking Him. Speak now my whole heart! Speak now to God, saying, I seek Thy face; Thy face, Lord, will I seek."*

May I ask you:

- Are you preoccupied with disturbing thoughts? Draw near to God.

- Does your job captivate your mind? Draw near to God.

- Are you burdened down with an overloaded schedule? Draw near to God.

How do you draw near to God? Find a quiet place, a closet, and throw out the clutter and shut the door. Draw near to God. Pull up a chair. Draw near to God.

Who is that before you now? Yes, you are right. It is God. He is drawing near to you; He is right there. That's Him! He has come just as He said. He has drawn near to you. He sits right there with you, waiting for you to speak.

So, open up, speak what is on your mind. You'll feel listened to because He cares for your soul.

One more thing, where light is, darkness cannot be. Satan has left because you have resisted him.

Submit yourselves therefore to God. *"Resist the devil, and he will flee from you. Draw near to God, and he will draw near to you."* **James 4:7-8 ESV**

Matthew 11:28-30 ESV: *"Come to me, all who labor and are heavy laden, and I will give you rest. Take my yoke upon you, and learn from me, for I am gentle and lowly in heart, and you will find rest for your souls. For my yoke is easy, and my burden is light."*
Think about it. *Selah!*

Day 84: Put On A Happy Face

"These things have I spoken to you, that my joy may be in you, and that your joy may be full." **John 15:11 ESV**

"Put on a Happy Face!" The lyrics of this song were written by Lee Adams and the music was composed by Charles Sprouse. It was used in the movie <u>Bye, Bye Birdie</u> in 1960 and sung as a duet by Dick Van Dyke and Janet Leigh. You can put on a happy face and not be happy, but if you are filled with joy, then the happy face is a reflection of your heart. You are actually and genuinely happy when you are filled with joy.

The Bible tells us in **Nehemiah 8:10** that the joy of the Lord is our strength and in **Psalm 16:11** that when we are in the presence of God there is fullness of joy. The angels told the shepherds in the field of Bethlehem that they had good news for them and that it contained great joy. The joy was that Jesus was born and in Him there is fullness of joy.

In Jesus there is exceeding great joy (**Psalm 43:4**). **Psalm 23:5** says that our cup overflows. Where Jesus is, there is joy. Joy trumps storms, trouble, and tragedy because it is our strength (**James 1:2**).

You can put on a happy face and not have joy, but when you are filled with joy, the happy face is the icon of the joy within you. Happiness is dependant upon joy. The happy face reflects undeniable joy. Jesus wants us to have joy, and we will have it if we are beside Jesus. In

Him there is fullness of joy. Joy exceeds mere happiness. It confirms our happy spirit. It explodes within us and consumes our countenance.

If your cup is full of joy, then there is no room for gloom. There is no place even for melancholy. Joy is beyond average. Joy is extravagant. It is extreme, and it is strong.

Think about it. *Selah!*

Day 85: What If You Lose Your Job?

"As for you, you meant evil against me, but God meant it for good, to bring it about that many people should be kept alive, as they are today. So do not fear; I will provide for you and your little ones. Thus he comforted them and spoke kindly to them."
Genesis 50:20-21 ESV

Do you worry about losing your job? Maybe you have already lost it and you just don't know what you are going to do. Maybe you lost it because of failures on your own, or maybe it was because of the callousness of another person's heart. It could be because of an unstable economic climate that has brought about the need for a cutback in the company in which you are employed.

To have a job is not a right that is owed to an individual. It is a blessing. No one deserves a job. A job is a task or service that someone needs to have done and is willing to pay another person a certain price to fulfill that task or service. If the need for the task declines or the service is no longer needed, the job will end. The problem is that all of us base our security in life on the job that we have and the person who has employed us to do those tasks and services.

Here is the bottom line: For the believer, we serve The Master, our God. He is the bottom line supplier of all that we need and if He has called us to an area of service, then He is going to provide for us. He can use the people, or corporations that we work for, or someone else or something else. He is the faithful one, not another.

If people scheme against you, God will not. If disease comes upon you, God will supply all that you need and sufficient grace for the moment. Joseph eased his scheming brothers when he responded to their fears, *"As for you, you meant evil against me, but God meant it for good, to bring it about that many people should be kept alive, as they are today. So do not fear; I will provide for you and your little ones. Thus he comforted them and spoke kindly to them."* **Genesis 50:20-21 ESV**

If you lose you job, don't lose your faith in God. Provide for others when God puts into your hand the means to provide. Don't get even. Be faithful. Don't worry about tomorrow; and when you have done all that you can do, let God do the rest. "When you've done your best, let God do the rest." Don't worry and fret over the things in which you have no control. It only causes you unnecessary harm. **Psalm 37:8**

You job as a believer is to make disciples where God has placed you, and He will reward you for your services in faithfully doing that task. God will supply all that you need according to his riches in heaven through Christ Jesus (**Philippians 4:19**).

Think about it. *Selah!*

Day 86: Is It Worth It?

"Yes, everything else is worthless when compared with the infinite value of knowing Christ Jesus my Lord. For his sake I have discarded everything else, counting it all as garbage, so that I could gain Christ." **Philippians 3:8 NLT**

Exodus 2 records the birth of Moses, and when we think about Moses we see a roller coaster life. We first think of a disadvantaged child. The writer of Hebrews says this about Moses in **Hebrews 11:23-26 ESV,** *"By faith Moses, when he was born, was hidden for three months by his parents, because they saw that the child was beautiful, and they were not afraid of the king's edict. By faith Moses, when he was grown up, refused to be called the son of Pharaoh's daughter, choosing rather to be mistreated with the people of God than to enjoy the fleeting pleasures of sin. He considered the reproach of Christ greater wealth than the treasures of Egypt, for he was looking to the reward."*

Paul testifies, as does Moses, that serving Christ is well worth all the stuff that life may throw at us. Remember, *"He considered the reproach of Christ greater wealth than the treasures of Egypt."* (**Hebrews 11:26**) and *"I have discarded everything else, counting it all as garbage, so that I could gain Christ"* (**Philippians 3:8 NLT**).

Now in our lives, we will be challenged with stuff that seeks to turn our eyes away from the Christ that we serve and attempt to refocus our eyes upon others who "seem" to be fairing better than we. But they are not. It is garbage when compared to life in Christ; it is merely temporary and not eternal. The treasures of heaven are of much greater value than anything on this earth.

Never give up, never give in, and always keep your eyes on Christ. He is worth it.

Think about it. *Selah!*

Day 87: Being The Right Person

"For the husband is the head of the wife even as Christ is the head of the church, his body, and is himself its Savior." **Ephesians 5:23 ESV**

In marriage, the desire ought to be to find "Mr. Right and Mrs. Right" and this requires each person to be a right person.

The Bible gives specific requirements for being "Mr. and Mrs. Right" but the difficulty is when we disagree with what God's Word says and when we are offended by what God's Word says.

Following requires a leader and a follower, and a good family needs a good leader and good followers. There is a chain of command in the family and the Bible way is this: The top leader is the Holy Spirit whom Jesus left as a guide, teacher, and comforter for us and to us. The next link in leadership in a loving and joyful family is the husband, then the wife, and then the children. It is these links that cause the Christian family to bow-up and question the chain of leadership that God desires and wills. We seem to accept the top links of Christ and the Holy Spirit but it just seems that way because we hesitate and question them. Perhaps it's because we feel slighted or overlooked. Perhaps it's because we feel we know better. The real difficulty, I believe, is that we have never actually tried to apply God's way in our family.

If you haven't tried it, may I suggest a few things I heard from Michael Guido. He lists a few things one ought to put in place in the home in order to have a home that is acceptable and right before God:

1.   Live in love. Love with the same love as Christ has loved his church.

2. Bear all things and forbear all things together. When we share a burden,
it is halved and when we share a joy the joy is doubled.

3. Be quick to give to each other and forgive each other.

4. Read and live God's Word together.

5. Live your lives together, do things with each other, and be best of friends.

6. Talk with each other; don't fight with each other.

7. Eat with each other and fast together.

8. Be purposeful and assertive in drawing near to each other and you will resist the pull of the Devil.

So if you are looking for Mr. and Mrs. Right, be right. If you question Mr. and Mrs. Right, ask God and He will reaffirm his Word in your family.
Think about it. *Selah!*

Day 88: A Pioneer

"Do you see what this means—all these pioneers who blazed the way, all these veterans cheering us on? It means we'd better get on with it. Strip down, start running—and never quit! No extra spiritual fat, no parasitic sins. Keep your eyes on Jesus, who both began and finished this race we're in." **Hebrews 12:1-2 The Message**

"The rivers may be wide, the mountains may be tall, we ain't afraid of man or beast we're trail blazers all." So goes "The Lord's Been Good to Me, The pioneer Song" in the Walt Disney <u>American Legends, Vol. 1</u> cartoon, "Johnny Appleseed."

Pioneers are encouragers, examples and models to help shape one's life. Our country has them, the church has them, and we find them in our families. These veterans give us strength to carry on in the midst of trouble. We think, *"If they can do it, so can I."*

The writer of Hebrews talks about the heroes of our faith, and then follows it with the example of a race and the crowd within the stadium cheering on the participants in the race. We need not consider what we do not have but what we have been promised and the one who promised. Look up to the face of the Master and you won't face disaster.

"Looking unto Jesus the author and finisher of our faith" (**Hebrews 12:2 KJV**). He is the Victor, the

Champion, the perfecter of our faith, and our God. *"Do you see what this means—all these pioneers who blazed the way, all these veterans cheering us on? It means we'd better get on with it* (**Hebrews 12:1 The Message**).

Think about it. *Selah!*

Day 89: Jesus Died Even For Them

"Or do you presume on the riches of his kindness and forbearance and patience, not knowing that God's kindness is meant to lead you to repentance." **Romans 2:4 ESV**

What comes to your mind when you hear the word, **ISIS**? What are your thoughts when you hear of the persecution of Christians in the country North Korea? If I were to bring up the subject of abortion and the selling of baby parts for medical research by professional, educated people, does that cause you to be enraged? These people certainly could be classified as ungodly.

I would say that the lightest words to be used would be swift justice and then quickly ratchet up to greater words of wrath. All of these deeds performed within society and Christianity in particular are revolting. It makes the believer see with accuracy the downward spiral of a sinful soul. It causes one to see the depth of a sinful soul on this earth. Our thoughts must also be: *"There go I but for the grace of God."*

The Apostle Paul writes in **Romans 5:20 KJV** *". . . But where sin abounded, grace did much more abound."* Jesus has called His followers to take His Good News to these people. We are to be witnesses and ambassadors for Him, not judge and jury. God is the judge, He is the jury, and He will carry out His verdict of eternal death.

Remember while we were still sinning, Christ died for us (**Romans 7:5; Ephesians 2:3**). God is rich in mercy, He overflows with grace, and He is filled with love and, therefore, He offers forgiveness for repentance of our sins, as we trust Him to be our Savior. That sounds unbelievable, but it is true. **2 Peter 3:9**

So, here is the point; be a witness and ambassador, not a judge and jury. *"Let him who is without sin among you be the first to throw a stone at her."* **John 8:7 ESV**

Think about it. *Selah!*

58239896R00120

Made in the USA
Charleston, SC
05 July 2016